BUILDING A VIBRANT COMMUNITY

HOW CITIZEN-POWERED CHANGE IS RESHAPING AMERICA

Quint Studer

Published by:

Be the Bulb Publishing

1947 Pine Ridge Drive

Janesville, WI 53545

608-757-1987

ISBN: 978-0-9981311-1-5

Library of Congress Control Number: 2018930857

Printed in the United States of America

To Vice Admiral Jack Fetterman and Mayor Emeritus Vince J. Whibbs Sr., thank you for your leadership. We continue to be inspired by the lessons you taught and the manner in which you lived.

"Wait…haven't I read this story already?"

We would be thrilled if you read this book straight through from Chapter 1 to Chapter 18 in sequential order. But we know people are busy and don't always do it that way. That's why we wrote *Building a Vibrant Community* to also function as a reference book of sorts. It's set up so you can jump right to whichever chapter you need in the moment. For this reason, cover-to-cover readers may find that certain facts and stories have been repeated to illustrate examples throughout the book. However you choose to read it, we're grateful. And we hope you'll find plenty of insights and advice that make your own journey go a bit more smoothly.

Table of Contents

Foreword

Sometimes what *should* be obvious turns out the most difficult to see.

This axiom has held true whether I find myself researching at the University of Chicago, giving economic advice to the president of the United States, or making business decisions as Uber's chief economist.

In the following pages, Quint Studer recognizes that every community wants to be a special place for its residents where safety and good jobs are afterthoughts.

Yet, Quint is also keenly aware that what most communities fall short on is understanding *how to achieve those aspirations.*

The *how* is the most difficult element to see.

Similar to a grand artist perfecting a masterpiece, Quint's broad strokes bring meaning and understanding to community revitalization.

Although I consider myself an expert on regional and urban economics and early childhood education, what is contained in this book cannot be found in the broader literatures.

This is because Quint's journey is unlike any other I know.

Born a bucolic in La Grange, IL, one would expect his partial deafness and speech impediment would never allow him out of the proverbial salt mines. Yet, his passions to help people, from those in need of special education to sputtering hospitals, gave Quint the breadth of knowledge to improve the world.

This book represents his efforts to continue that transformation. While drawing from lessons learned on his personal journey, Quint summarizes a playbook on how communities can move toward vibrancy, step by step.

One will not find this knowledge in the social theories of economic growth; rather these are gems only a worn tool would know.

What I found quite compelling are the various strategies that leverage behavioral economics and psychological insights to alleviate fear amongst community members, garner confidence, and manage the psychological hurdles that every community faces to achieve greatness.

What was equally as engaging were the decades of know-how on avoiding critical mistakes, the key element of "downtown" in community structure, and the role of small business as change makers. Indeed, the empirical evidence from the academy fully supports Quint's conjecture that small business owners are the catalysts for real change and broad community empowerment.

While I was moved by all of these insights, what I found most inspiring were two other elements of the book: first, the role of government.

Mounting budgetary difficulties of federal and state governments in the United States and of decentralized governments in a number of countries have generated a serious concern with the problem of intergovernmental fiscal relations. In the United States, President Reagan called for a "new federalism" approach in the early 1980s that was characterized by heavy reliance on state and local fiscal decisions.

Analyzing the appropriate division of functions among levels of government is an age-old economics topic, but one that can gain from an understanding of elements in these pages. In this way, the wisdom in this tome can extend well beyond the community striving for excellence; it can help to inform the next generation of academicians and policymakers interested in further devolution.

The second element I was most deeply moved by is the critical importance that Quint places on education, particularly early education. This is where Quint's work to make his home community, Pensacola, America's first "Early Learning City" comes into the community development picture.

Educational disparities are one of the most significant public policy issues of our time, particularly in the United States. The question as to why the substantial resources that have been committed to public education over the past half century have had seemingly little effect on closing the achievement gap remains unresolved. One key feature of the educational expenditure pattern, however, is that it has focused on remediation rather than prevention.

In my work with Dana Suskind, we have focused on three distinct features of the policy problem. First, by focusing public policy dollars on prevention rather than remediation, we call for much earlier educational programs than currently conceived. Second, our approach has parents at the center of the education production function rather than at its periphery. Third, we advocate attacking the macro education problem using a public health methodology, rather than focusing on piecemeal advances.

This book complements our vision of early childhood education by providing the necessary set of tools and instruments for communities to flourish.

Sometimes what *should* be obvious turns out the most difficult to see.

—John A. List
Chairman, Department of Economics, University of Chicago
Chief Economist, Uber

CHAPTER 1

Introduction

Thank you for reading *Building a Vibrant Community*. If you look at the cover, you'll see the subtitle of this book is *How Citizen-Powered Change Is Reshaping America*. It's really happening. We live in exciting times. Communities across the country are making big changes for the better, and if you're reading this, *yours* probably is, too. My hope is that when you finish this book you'll have a game plan. You'll know what you're already doing really, really well and you'll feel good about it. And hopefully, you'll have learned a few new tips that might help take you and your community to the next level.

In Thomas L. Friedman's book *Thank You for Being Late: An Optimist's Guide to Thriving in the Age of Accelerations*, he talks about how rapid accelerations in technology, globalization, and Mother Nature are disrupting our lives and leaving people feeling destabilized. He says these forces are like a hurricane, one in which the winds of change are swirling so fast that families can't find a way to anchor themselves. Friedman makes the case that the only answer is building healthy communities, ones that are flexible enough to navigate this hurricane and provide stability for the citizens within them. He quotes the words from a ballad by Brandi Carlile, "You can dance in a hurricane, but only if you're standing in the eye." He says the "eye" in this hurricane must be our local communities. We must provide people a firm place to stand and find stability while all this change is swirling around us.

According to Friedman, healthy communities not only help get citizens stabilized (economically and emotionally), but they are the key to repairing our nation. Existing power structures have aged out. Institutions have broken down. Things are a mess. He says the solutions to all our big problems reside at the local level, where there is enough nimbleness to adapt to changes. We often look to government to solve the big problems, but he says government simply can't move swiftly enough to be effective by themselves.

Michael Bloomberg and Carl Pope released a book titled *Climate of Hope: How Cities, Businesses, and Citizens Can Save the Planet*. In their book, they make the case that climate change is not one big problem but rather a series of smaller problems. We can tackle these problems. But by "we," Bloomberg and Pope don't mean national governments. They mean local leaders—elected officials, CEOs of corporations, small business owners, and citizens who care enough to take action. These are the people who can defeat climate change. And in the process they can create a stronger economy and healthier citizens.

I read both of these books with great interest. The idea that we needed to create healthy, vibrant communities in order to help our citizens thrive and reach their potential, and that we needed to engage local solutions to combat our biggest problems, really resonated with me. Shifting the thinking from global to a local focus made perfect sense and was very much in line with what we have been and are experiencing in Pensacola, FL.

Pensacola had experienced several decades of economic decline and had been ravaged by a hurricane. As a community, we had been suffering in a big way. In addition to economic and infrastructure problems, we were experiencing a talent drain. Our young people were leaving for better opportunities. We recognized that we had to do something and do it quickly. Through a series of local initiatives, we had experienced a citizen-led change and revitalization that was in full swing when these two books came out. After nearly 13 years of rebuilding, we have really seen big progress. Pensacola is living proof that healthy communities are the key to their own economic revival and that local solutions are the answer.

A strong local community has always been vital, but now quality communities matter more than ever. People have always wanted great places to live, with a solid local economy, good schools for their children, and fun activities nearby, but we had stopped being intentional about preserving our neighborhoods and local communities. The economic, social, and political challenges we've faced over the last couple of decades have driven home how important our communities really are.

Functioning communities are important on many levels. The breakdown of our cities has other ramifications. Our bodies aren't working. We depend too much on cars, and our sedentary lifestyles are killing us. Social relations aren't working. We need and want to be connected. Politics aren't working. The revenue model doesn't make sense. Conversations aren't working. We aren't working together as a community to solve neighborhood problems.

Great communities make us feel grounded, protected, and empowered. They provide jobs and solid economic growth. They attract new talent and keep existing talent from leaving town. They do a great job of educating young people, they provide safe neighborhoods, and they nurture the health and well-being of all citizens. They provide a sense of belonging, connection, and support. And they're just more fun to live in.

Every community has the potential to be great. Geographic location helps, but it's only one small piece of the puzzle.

The good news is that quality communities can be built. The operative word is "built." Great communities don't just happen on their own. They are created strategically and intentionally. And they are almost always created through local solutions.

The methodology from the Gates Foundation is very clear. It is simple and stuck with me: Create a prototype to test a new approach. Record processes. Document findings. Tweak methods. Replicate successes. This is the path we took in rebuilding Pensacola. We are by no means finished, but we've learned a lot on this journey. Our hope is that other communities can utilize some of the ideas and craft their own framework for creating their own healthy community, as we have learned from others. When the lives of all our citizens are better, we are better.

CHAPTER 2

The Pensacola Story

Often the dots don't get connected until a journey is far down the road or even over. Only in hindsight can one look back and clearly see the path that was taken to get there. There had been many attempts to revitalize Pensacola over the years. Like most communities, there were many government-sponsored plans, chamber plans, etc. Also, like many, they are very hard to execute for a number of reasons. These can range from lack of funds to stakeholder disagreements to election cycles to overall economic changes. The process described in this book included all of these challenges—and even more.

My involvement was purely accidental. In a way, this was an advantage, because I didn't come into the process with a lot of rigid ideas on how things should be done. This made me more flexible and more open to taking risks. I never knew how tough it would be; if I had, I probably never would have tried. This task is not for the faint-hearted or weak-kneed. If you are reading this book, you already have what it takes: passion and a willingness to learn.

Now that things are well underway, it's easier to look back and see what worked and what didn't work—and to share what we've learned so far, both wins and losses, with other communities. That's why this book was written.

Taking time to tell our story made it very clear that there are certain ingredients that help communities become vibrant. (By *vibrant* I mean a place where young people can stay home after college and still fulfill their potential, a place that attracts talent and private investments, a place where a strong tax base leads to financial health. A place that's safe and clean with a great education system.)

What are these needed ingredients? There are the people who want something better for their children and grandchildren. There is the willingness to look at data objectively. There are outside circumstances that present themselves. There are people from outside the community who become key mentors. There are times when the right actions are taken, as well as times when things just don't go as planned. In the journey to create a more vibrant community, no one goes undefeated. There are wins and losses along the way.

We can see things now that we couldn't see in the beginning. If someone had told me in the early 2000s that I'd be involved in community revitalization and eventually write a book about it, I certainly would have doubted it. Not that I wasn't interested in writing books; I've written seven of them on leadership and creating better organizations and better employees. I'd worked with my own company in helping organizations achieve high performance. But none of my previous experience or skill set could be directly applied to improving a community, or so it seemed.

As it turned out, my background had actually prepared me well for this journey. I just didn't realize it at the time it all began.

Business and Baseball

On June 9, 1996, I arrived in Pensacola to be the administrator of Baptist Hospital. I had spent the past three years in Chicago working in healthcare, and before that, a number of years in Wisconsin. We had some success, and I was recruited to Baptist to improve their performance. To do so it was apparent that we had to create a great place for employees to work, patients to receive care, and physicians to practice medicine. We had to create a culture of high performance.

Building on what I had learned before coming to Pensacola, and because we had a great team at the hospital, we achieved success. The success attracted the attention of other healthcare systems that were interested in adopting many of the practices. So in 2000, I left Baptist to start my own company. We wanted our offices to be close to where our children went to school, so we rented office space in Gulf Breeze, FL, a small community just east of Pensacola. We recruited great employees, and the company grew quickly.

Many of the skills I learned during this time in my life—managing change, responding to changes in the external environment, engaging employees, creating great customer service, and so forth—prepared me for what we would eventually do in our efforts to make Pensacola better. In many ways I have found that changing the culture of a community is not so different from changing the culture of an organization.

In 2002, my wife, Rishy, and I bought an independent baseball team, the Pensacola Pelicans. At that time it played at Pensacola Junior College, which is now Pensacola State College. In 2003 the team moved to the University of West Florida, which is a school about 20 minutes north of downtown Pensacola. (Bear with me because this baseball connection turns out to be really important to Pensacola's story.)

The Meeting That Kicks Off the Journey

Then in early 2004, Tom Bonfield, the city manager of Pensacola, called and asked me to breakfast. Tom explained that he was curious if we were open to moving the company from Gulf Breeze to downtown Pensacola. He shared that many companies had moved out or closed and he was very interested in bringing our growing company downtown.

In that same conversation, we talked about the Pensacola Pelicans. Tom shared the possibility of creating a place downtown where the team could play.

My company was really interested in the idea of moving downtown. We looked at some existing office space, but it became apparent that a new building would work best for our needs. Also, the idea of putting a stadium in downtown Pensacola intrigued me. So in an effort to learn more, a team of experts was put together to help assess the idea of constructing a new building and a stadium.

This team consisted of Miller Caldwell Jr., an architect, Dick Appleyard and Ellis Bullock, who each owned marketing and advertising companies, Raad Cawthon, who worked for Ellis, Mort O'Sullivan, an owner of an accounting firm, and Bob Hart, an attorney. I had a good working relationship with all of them, and they were well respected. (Interestingly enough, this "steering committee" turned out to be instrumental as things started to unfold.) We contracted with Mike Thiessen of The Madison Group, who had a lot of experience in helping other communities build stadiums and who brought outside expertise to the situation.

In looking to build a stadium for the Pelicans, we had commissioned some schematic drawings. These included a multi-use park, an office building, and some land that could also be used for other offices and retail space. We found a large piece of acreage just west of downtown, the EPA Superfund American Creosote Works Inc. site that was sitting vacant and had been for years. It had suffered significant environmental damage, and we had Mort determine if it made sense financially to try to recapture the property. Turns out, the land was just not suitable because of the environmental issues, so we put the project on pause.

Around the same time, Jim Clifton, chairman and CEO of Gallup, contacted me. Gallup does considerable work in healthcare. He had noticed that organizations served by my company performed well. Being a person always searching for solutions, Jim invited me to come meet with him in Washington, DC. While we spent most of the time discussing healthcare, he happened to mention that Gallup had completed a study on economic development and why some cities thrive and others do not. He shared the findings with me that later went on to become the foundation of his book *The Coming Jobs War.*

My take on what Jim shared was that the key to thriving is not location, nor is it the type of government structure. Rather, a community's likelihood of thriving comes down to several factors that all need to come together in the right way at the right times.

One is its ability to identify and keep those companies that get their revenue from *outside* the community. This means new dollars are coming into the area, rather than the same dollars just being moved around in the community. He said if you want to know how your elected officials are doing, just ask them to name ten companies that get their revenue from outside of town, and ask what they're doing to keep them. He also shared stories of companies that had relocated, and when they were asked why they moved, they said it was because the new city was spending a lot more time trying to recruit them than their current community was spending trying to keep them. Retention is just as important as recruitment.

Another factor is the community's skill in identifying and helping promising start-up companies. Due to the nature of many companies, owners often need creative ways to get this start-up capital. Today's banking environment makes it hard for small businesses to get start-up loans. A community that can help them get that needed capital is more likely to thrive. Once again he advised going to the elected officials, or the people in charge of economic development, and asking what five or ten start-up companies in their community might grow if they had more capital. Communities benefit when local companies sprout and start growing.

Another very important factor is a vibrant downtown. Jim explained that communities really benefit from a vibrant downtown, as it creates tax dollars and keeps talent in the area. The vertical growth that happens in vibrant downtowns pays for urban sprawl.

A big takeaway from this meeting was that four elements are needed to create a vibrant downtown. They are as follows: programming that brings lots of people downtown on a regular basis, retail and entertainment options, office space options, and diverse residential options. While it would be nice to get the residential first so the retail and entertainment can do better, that can't always happen. Often the residential part is hardest, because people want to live in places where they can shop, work, and play.

The first priority is getting the downtown programmed. People expect retailers or restaurants to just pop up downtown, but that's not how it works. Businesses follow people. So getting people downtown on a regular basis, not just once in a while, is vital. Most communities don't have the dollars to make large, permanent investments to get people downtown right away. You can draw people downtown with smaller, less formal gatherings to get things rolling. Farmers markets, food and art festivals, food trucks, concerts, gallery nights, etc. all work really well.

Once people are coming downtown on a regular basis, traffic to restaurants and shops will pick up. When that happens, more people are coming downtown, so office space becomes more attractive. People like to work downtown when there are lots of things to do.

A key element is to offer a variety of residential options. If there is not a stable residential foundation downtown, the community gets very dependent on the state of the economy. When the economy gets tough, non-residents stop coming to bars and restaurants. This is less likely to happen if they live nearby. A major residential presence downtown is the fourth leg of the stool. It really keeps the community from swinging back and forth with the economy.

A bonanza for a downtown is a major presence by a university. Universities actually do better than most in down economies, which creates more stability. Of course, the other great thing about having a university or college downtown is that they provide a lot of intellectual capital and often turn out entrepreneurs. Pensacola, like many other communities, does not have that. However, we keep trying.

I learned a lot from Jim Clifton, and we will talk about all of these insights in more detail throughout the book. One thing's for sure, though: Meeting him was a pivotal coincidence in a whole string of them. In this journey, timing was everything. Certain people, places, and events just came together at the right time. Looking back, I can see how all the pieces fit together, and meeting Jim at that particular time was a seminal moment.

The Wheels Start Turning

Jim really got me thinking about how communities are developed and really paying attention to the cities and towns I traveled to. I had been spending a lot of time on the road and of course had experienced many communities. Some were much more vibrant than others. I was in two or three different cities every week, and I'd certainly noticed that some were a lot more fun to be in than others. Some had a lot of great restaurants, a lot of things to do, and a feeling of energy. Others seemed to roll up the streets at night. But until I met Jim, I had not put much thought into why.

So while I didn't quite realize it at the time, a lot of different circumstances were coming together. If you are reading this book, maybe this is happening to you, too. Anyway, my mind was racing. I had really started thinking about the possibilities for Pensacola.

Upon getting back to Gulf Breeze, I called Randy Hammer. At the time, Randy was the editor of the *Pensacola News Journal.* He was aware of the conversations we were having about developing downtown and was very interested in my meeting with Jim Clifton. I sent him the material Jim had given me. He read it and said, "We need to bring Jim Clifton to Pensacola to do a presentation on how to grow a community." He also said, "You need to connect with Dr. Ken Ford; he is interested in this as well."

Dr. Ford is founder and CEO of the Florida Institute for Human & Machine Cognition (IHMC)—a not-for-profit research institute affiliated with the State University System of Florida that studies robotics, artificial intelligence, and other areas of technology—which was doing a monthly series of community lectures. I spoke to him about bringing Jim Clifton to Pensacola to speak. Ken wanted to make our downtown better because it was a challenge to attract talent for IHMC. The type of talent he needed to recruit liked being able to work, live, and play downtown. So we ended up booking Jim in advance for the November 2004 lecture.

This talent issue had really caught my attention. It suddenly seemed very clear that a vibrant downtown could have a huge effect on Pensacola's business community, economy in general, and our quality of life. I really value expertise and was interested in learning who might be able to help us. Ken suggested calling Ray Gindroz, co-founder of a company out of Pittsburgh called Urban Design Associates. Ken had brought Ray to Pensacola earlier and had some thoughts on revitalization.

A Hurricane Levels Our Plans (Or Does It?)

A vibrant Pensacola didn't seem like just an idea anymore. It felt like something that could happen, and was, in fact, already happening in some small ways. And then disaster struck. On September 16, 2004, Hurricane Ivan roared through Pensacola.

The hurricane caused major damage. Roads, bridges, and commercial and residential buildings were destroyed. Everywhere you looked you saw blue tarps on roofs, and many residences had been completely destroyed. FEMA trailers were everywhere. Because a local sewage treatment plant had overflowed, raw sewage had encroached into homes and businesses.

All of this led to a major rebuilding challenge for northwest Florida. Suddenly, just as we were on the cusp of change, everyone's life was thrown topsy-turvy and—just like that—we were back to food, clothing, and shelter. People were in survival mode, literally, and they desperately wanted life to just get back to normal.

As you can imagine, this set things back. The revitalization plans had come to a sudden halt.

Shortly after the hurricane, a group of community leaders came together to discuss the rebuilding process. This group, which I was not a member of, researched what other communities had done after such a catastrophe. It turned out that in addition to finding people places to live, filing insurance claims, getting roads and bridges open, etc., others had used their situation to launch a large community project. For example, the city of Homestead had done this back in 1992 in the aftermath of Hurricane Andrew. The idea is that such a project serves as evidence that a community is overcoming the challenge and moving forward. Some people from the strategic planning committee were at this meeting and started thinking that our project (the one that was on pause at the moment) might be the kind of thing that could bring the community together, and the time might be right to launch.

So all these things started coming together. We realized that the hurricane had not stopped the plans after all. It was not a roadblock but an opportunity. In fact, it had become the springboard for bringing big, real, meaningful change to Pensacola. The time was right to make it all happen.

A Waterfront Park Is Born

During these hurricane meetings, it came up that there had been a discussion about an office building and a stadium for the Pelicans but we were having trouble finding the right property. At the same time, someone mentioned that Vice Admiral Jack Fetterman, who was president and CEO of the Naval Aviation Museum Foundation and a well-respected member of the community, was also working on a project. He had an idea for creating a downtown maritime museum to highlight the area's rich maritime history. He felt with an additional attraction many of the 700,000 National Naval Aviation Museum visitors would stay an additional night and this would help Pensacola. We both made presentations to the group, and it was suggested that our projects complemented each other and that we should find a way to partner.

As it happened, Admiral Fetterman and I decided to combine the projects. We reconstituted the old workgroup. We also brought in Mayor Emeritus Vince J. Whibbs Sr., who was another community icon, and Dr. John Cavanaugh, the president of the University of West Florida. Dr. Cavanaugh wanted to bring the school's history, marine biology, and archeology departments onsite as well. The idea was that having the university there would help attract matching funds to help build the maritime museum. Tom Bonfield was very excited about the possibility. He also stated it was vital that private citizens lead this effort, because the government had led a recent effort to build a new auditorium, but the city council's approval was overturned by a citizen referendum after site preparation had already begun. So he really pushed the fact that he supported it, but private people would have to lead it.

As we started talking about a location for the project, Jack suggested a waterfront piece of property called Trillium, which the city had purchased in 2000 for $3.63 million. This 27.5-acre parcel of land had served as a fuel terminal in the past but had sat vacant for more than ten years. It was overgrown and contaminated. The soil would need to be cleaned up before anything could be built there.

I was skeptical about this idea. The fact that the soil needed remediation was only part of the problem. A few years earlier, the city had approved a $40-million project for the site that included an auditorium and a park, but a referendum led by Councilman Marty Donovan (the sole dissenting city council member) had overturned the vote in 2003. I was nervous about taking on the controversy, but the Admiral wasn't afraid of anything, so off we went.

This was early 2005. At the time, the country was financially strong, but not Pensacola. Tax dollars had been flat. Now, I wanted to do a gut check: *Did this project make sense? Would it be financially worth it for the city? Would it really increase private downtown investment?* I wanted to dig deeper. I remembered Dr. Ford suggesting Ray Gindroz, the urban planner from Pittsburgh. A group of us flew to Pittsburgh to meet with him. It was valuable for he had recently worked in the city. After looking over the city maps and financials and hearing our description of the project, Gindroz started sharing what he had seen in other cities. He was very positive about the project. In talking with him, he also shared other tactics for creating a vibrant downtown, including slowing traffic downtown, making the city more walkable, and building foot traffic, etc. He was a wealth of information.

When we came back from Pittsburgh, the preliminary project plans, including financing, were put in place. The proposed Community Maritime Park would include a stadium (which would also be a venue for other community events) and a maritime museum. All of this would be built along the Pensacola Bay's edge.

At a cost of $70.7 million, this would be the largest public-private partnership in Pensacola's history. Of the total amount, $29.1 million could come from the private sector. Here is where the private sector funding would come from: Rishy and I committed $15 million to the project and Jack promised to raise $12.8 million for the maritime museum. The rest of the private sector funding would come from commercial leases. That left $41.6 million to be funded by the public through city bond financing, state grants, and the New Markets Tax Credit Program. The existing dedicated tax revenue from the Community Redevelopment Agency (CRA), which governed the downtown tax increment financing (TIF) district, as well as anticipated growth in tax revenues within the district would be the ancillary generator of funds to pay off the bonds.

Our project team started pitching the city council in late 2004. We had the support of City Manager Tom Bonfield and city CFO Dick Barker, and the next step was the city council. We met individually with each council member and shared the research and project details. When the city council finally voted, it passed 8 to 1. Everyone was in favor except for one person, Councilman Marty Donovan.

Trials and Tragedies

The fact that Marty Donovan wasn't supportive was not a surprise, as he had helped defeat the previous proposal for the Trillium site. In fact, he got that group revved up again, and they began fighting this one, too. He collected signatures and forced a referendum to try to overturn the city council's vote. This process took nearly a year and it was an extremely difficult time. Emotions ran high, both pro and con. Although the *Pensacola News Journal* and the *Independent News* ran major stories on what we were trying to do—and a lot of feedback to them was quite favorable—the opposition was also fierce. We learned just how difficult it is to move projects forward. But this time the results would be different.

We brought in Bruce Barcelo, a public opinion research specialist. We felt it was important to have good, objective data. In situations like this, it's not uncommon for people to generalize, exaggerate, over-emphasize, or sometimes even misrepresent or be confused as to what the community members really want.

Bruce helped us make sense of what the numbers were really saying. He was instrumental in collecting data about what people really wanted and he helped us figure out what the issues really were for the community. He came back to us with critical information like "people want access to water" or "people want their children to stay home." This helped shape the plan.

During this long process, we brought Ray Gindroz of Urban Design Associates to town to facilitate many community input sessions and to help educate people on such projects. He and his staff led several focus groups. While most people liked the idea of taking unusable land and making it accessible, the idea of a downtown stadium was what resonated with them pro and con. (The museum was not part of the vote since it was to be completely privately funded, as was the office building.)

We also used that time with Ray to learn more about city development. He shared many things that are in this book as well as other lessons learned. For example, he said that every downtown needed a great intersection, and we did not have one. He also reinforced that the key is to have fewer traffic lanes, not more, and to slow down traffic. Furthermore, he explained how downtowns die. He said that when malls open, many downtowns lose retailers. In those empty downtown spaces come tenants who may have paid rent, but do not create foot traffic. Therefore, other retailers leave. This creates a death spiral. Those lessons from Ray are a major part of this book.

It became clear the Community Maritime Park would help, but it would not be enough. Downtown needed to be revitalized, and that meant more programming.

As this was taking place, I stayed in touch with Randy Hammer. He was now the CEO of the newspaper in Asheville, NC, and he invited our workgroup to make a visit to benchmark the progress of his new hometown. When we arrived, I quickly became overwhelmed and maybe somewhat depressed. Downtown Asheville was amazing. What I saw was so great I could not fathom us ever achieving a downtown like that.

We were fortunate to get the perspective of several of the people who had been intimately involved in revitalizing downtown Asheville, including Rick Lutovsky, CEO at the time of the Asheville Area Chamber of Commerce, and Pat Whalen, president of Public Interest Projects Inc. We also spent some time with

Chuck Tessier, a commercial real estate developer, and his wife, Karen, who owned Market Connections, a marketing and public relations company in Asheville.

Thankfully they showed us lots of before pictures from the 1980s, which looked much like Pensacola did in the early 2000s: lots of empty buildings. They encouraged us and shared tactics very similar to those we had heard about from Jim Clifton and Ray Gindroz.

One of the key components of Asheville's success was their investment in small businesses and start-ups. Greg Walker Wilson, who at the time was CEO of Mountain BizWorks, a not-for-profit community development organization that helps fund, seed, and grow small businesses, explained how they systematically funded and mentored small businesses. They not only helped them get off the ground, but helped them grow and stay healthy. (Wilson has gone on to start his own consulting firm.)

We learned so much from this visit. Asheville gave us a chance to really experience a vibrant downtown.

There were a few other cities we benchmarked as well: Charleston, SC; Greenville, SC; Savannah, GA; Beloit, WI; and Portland, ME. These cities have been so helpful to Pensacola on our journey, and we're indebted to them. This is why we love hosting visitors who can learn from us.

During this time, sadly, Admiral Fetterman became ill. He passed away on March 24, 2006. The leadership baton was passed to former Mayor Whibbs. And just two months later, the mayor suffered a heart attack and died in his home.

Between the losses of these two visionaries and the struggle to get our proposal passed, this was a really painful time. I was learning a huge lesson in how politics work. This was going to take a lot of time, lots of money, and thick skin. By now, it was more than a park project. It was whether Pensacola was going to remain stuck as a city of potential or if that potential was going to be maximized.

One of the things that kept us going was watching the engagement level of a few of the community groups. The Pensacola Young Professionals (PYP) played a big role. This was a group of young people who got together and got super-involved in the process. They felt like they had a big stake in the outcomes. We were also inspired by how engaged our minority community was in the process. Juanita Scott, Audra Carter, Leroy Williams, Lumon May, and his brother, LuTimothy, worked nonstop in getting the minority community involved.

For both of these groups, their role was critical, as they were instrumental in getting people engaged. They walked the streets, pounded the pavement, and got the message out. They all spent countless hours educating people about the issues, answering questions, and getting people out to the polls to actually vote.

They have always cared deeply about the community, and this just further ignited their passion. They were inspired to see that they could really make a difference and that things were starting to happen. Ten years later a lot of these PYP people are community activists and are running their own businesses. So their experience with PYP set the stage for other projects. Lumon May went on to become one of the five elected commissioners for Escambia County.

Finally, the Referendum Passes

On September 5, 2006, after a long, hard battle, the referendum for the Vince J. Whibbs Sr. Community Maritime Park came to be. In the end, 9,842 approved the park (56 percent) and 7,701 voted no (44 percent). Of the 37,555 eligible voters, 17,500 cast ballots, a 46.6 percent turnout.

This was a defining moment in Pensacola's history. When one looks at Charleston, they will share that the development of the waterfront park was their defining moment. In Montgomery, they say it's when they put a ballpark on the river. This was to be our defining moment.

What won it was not baseball, but the idea that a vibrant community would keep their kids at home. It was a sign that maybe their children would not have to leave town, and children and grandchildren who had already moved away might come back. This was the message we kept at the forefront of all of our conversations with the community. It was the *why* behind everything we proposed and everything they voted for.

Creating a vibrant community is like throwing pebbles in a pond. While each pebble may not make a big splash, each one impacts the water, which creates ripples, which creates more ripples, which changes the pond. All are connected. So too are many actions in a community.

So after the referendum passed, the city created a community board to oversee the project, and the massive task of clearing away the toxic soil from the Trillium site began.

As this was evolving, the University of West Florida was reconsidering its part in the project. With Jack Fetterman's passing, the yeoman's work was being done by his widow, Nancy Fetterman, and many others. Dr. John Cavanaugh, the university president who was initially involved in the project, had left for another position. Dr. Judith Bense, the new university president, felt that while the money was there to build the maritime museum, sustaining it operationally might not be in the best interest of fiscal stewardship. It turned out that the state matching funds the university had been counting on were not available after all. By then, the onset of the Great Recession had gutted state revenues. So she decided not to move ahead with the museum.

I have come to understand and respect that decision more and more each year. I think it was a wise one. Too many times projects are built because the money is there for the building phase yet they struggle because they are not able to operate financially without large subsidies. UWF made the right call for them at the time.

Revitalizing 27 acres of contaminated soil and preparing to build a stadium takes a long time. Also, there were various obstacles and delays. As a result, the stadium that was supposed to open in 2009 didn't open until 2012.

Enter the Blue Wahoos

In December 2010, Rishy and I purchased a Double-A affiliated baseball team. The team was the Carolina Mudcats, located in Zebulon, NC. It's very hard to purchase a team that can be relocated due to lease issues. The Zebulon lease called for the owners of the Mudcats to make sure an affiliated team was there. So to move the Mudcats, a replacement team needed to be found for them. Steve Bryant, from whom I purchased the Mudcats, led a group to purchase a Single-A team that kept the Mudcats name, which could be moved to Zebulon. This freed up the Double-A franchise, so the Double-A team could move to Pensacola. This process was very hard. For Pensacola, this was a big win. It brought more credibility to the park and a 70-game schedule versus 48 (independent team), as well as a jolt of self-esteem for the community. Please don't think a stadium or a baseball team is a must. It is different for each community. What is a must are actions that bring lots of people downtown.

Sports and other community events are not only great economic drivers for development, they also bring the community together in neat ways. It can become a vehicle for citizens to strike up a conversation with the person next to them. It can serve as common ground for people of all walks of life to get to know each other. It truly helps build a sense of community and gives people a chance to connect.

With the park project well underway, we continued to think about everything we'd learned from Jim Clifton, Ray Gindroz, and Asheville. Our real goal was not to build a park but to increase tax revenue in the Escambia County Community Redevelopment Agency and to revitalize a downtown to attract and keep talent in the area. And so we kept the ball rolling. The more we learned, the more determined we were.

Sizing Up Downtown

We began putting a lot of energy into working on downtown Pensacola, particularly its main street, Palafox. While there were bars and restaurants, jewelers and art galleries, and a few retail spots, there were too many vacant storefronts and few good places to hang around on certain nights. Many of the streets were deserted on weekends. On a scale of 1 to 10, I believe most would have rated our downtown a 4 or 5.

While downtown Pensacola had much to be desired, there was also much to build on. The Davis, Elebash, and Meadows families still had their jewelry stores downtown. Now they've been joined by Susan Campbell Jewelry. A bit further south on Palafox there was Don Alans clothing store. Off Palafox was a lively entertainment spot called Seville Quarter as well as a historic district. Pensacola is fortunate to have a symphony, a chorus, a ballet, and an opera, as well as two theatres (Saenger Theatre and Pensacola Little Theatre). The Merrill family had opened Jackson's Steakhouse, and there was the Global Grill restaurant, as well as the bars New York Nick's and Intermission.

These were some of the bright spots. I would be remiss not to mention a few trailblazers. Deborah Dunlap and Clark Thompson were working hard to keep downtown Pensacola alive. Deborah had purchased some buildings and did a great job getting them to look great. Clark kept the existing office space active as best he could. Ray Russenberger had also invested farther south on Palafox near the water. So, building on the dedication of these folks, we went to work.

To demonstrate our commitment to downtown, Rishy and I purchased a large office building of around 44,000 square feet, the Rhodes Building, and did some minor remodeling. While it was located a bit farther north on Palafox than we would have preferred, it was important to show our confidence in downtown. Since then, a young mover and shaker, Chad Henderson, who owns a company called Catalyst HRE, has purchased the building and moved their corporate headquarters to the top floor. This is one of those great companies that brings revenue from outside the area but is invested in people and facilities here.

Working Toward a More Inclusive Pensacola

Rishy and I went to an event called the Goombay Festival located in what at the time was the center of the historic black district. It is the intersection of Belmont and DeVilliers. While at one time this had been a busy place, it was now facing major struggles. The festival was a group attempt to grow interest in the neighborhood, which is an example of Jim Clifton's programming story come to life.

On one corner was a vacant two-story building in desperate need of repair. The last store there was Gussie's Record Shop. Across the street was a three-story office building with very few tenants. On the third corner was a bottle club, which is where people come to keep drinking after the bars close. On the fourth corner was a large building that had multiple uses over the years.

Rishy noticed the empty building that was the record shop. We could see loose bricks at the top of the building and were worried they would fall and hurt someone. We also have a fondness for old buildings, and this one reminded us of Chicago, where we had once lived. Remembering our Asheville trip, we thought about renovating the building, helping a start-up, and focusing on inclusion. Our research had shown that Pensacola had a real shortage of minority-owned businesses. So, this project could give us a chance to achieve multiple goals.

First, we bought the building. We got in touch with a contractor we had used before called Napier Inc. and asked them to partner with a minority-owned contractor called May's Construction (owned by Lumon May), with a focus on minority workers on the project. We then looked for a minority chef who wanted to open a restaurant. We found a man named Cecil Johnson, who owned a very small restaurant in another part of town. We visited him and shared the idea of a restaurant on the corner of Belmont and DeVilliers.

One of the things we learned from Asheville was that start-ups need more than space; they might also need a little help. To make it work, we put into place some Asheville lessons. We purchased all the equipment, renovated the building (including two upstairs apartments), and created a lease with rent that moved up and down based on revenue. Cecil opened Five Sisters Blues Café, named after his sisters' recipes. Due to his hard work and great food, the place was an instant hit. More people came to that area.

After five years Cecil was ready to retire. We purchased the restaurant business from him and sold it to another local minority owner, Jean Pierre N'Dione. It continues today and has helped rebirth the neighborhood.

We have learned that once an investment is made, what takes place around it is key. Pensacola has vague zoning regulations—they don't spell out where retail stores go, where entertainment establishments go, or where restaurants go the way many vibrant communities do. We wanted to take steps to protect our investment. One solution is to partner with someone who owns adjacent property, so you can better manage the growth. So a few years after Five Sisters was up and running, we purchased the office building across the street. Eddie Todd Jr., an architect and a real leader in the community, owned some land next to the building. He agreed to combine his lots into the project to create a partnership called DeVilliers Square.

The inside was upgraded, as well as the lighted parking lot. Today the building is full. Driving into the neighborhood, you will see a flurry of residential units being built. There are also a few retail shops with more to come as well as the famous Blue Dot hamburger joint, a long-time Pensacola staple.

We learned once programs are in place to bring people to the area, then retail will come, then entertainment will come, then office space will come, then residential will come. That's what happened at Belmont and DeVilliers, and it started to thrive.

One Great Intersection

As Ray Gindroz mentioned, every great city needs a great intersection, and Pensacola didn't have one. There was an intersection at Palafox and Garden that was a possibility, but Ray said it wasn't the best choice. The road had four lanes, and there was a big median, so it just wasn't right. He had also taught us about traffic patterns and said the idea is to slow down traffic, not speed it up.

He drew attention to the intersection at Palafox and Main. At the time, it had two empty lots and two buildings that had been vacant a long time. It soon became clear that this needed to be the focus for creating a great intersection.

As we were thinking about all this, Rishy and I were driving through the Palafox and Main intersection and began to pay attention to the two empty buildings. Rishy had been to North Carolina and had seen an olive oil store she just loved. She thought it would be neat to have an olive oil store in downtown Pensacola and she realized this was the perfect spot for the store. So we bought one of these buildings, renovated it, and opened a store called the Bodacious Olive. Later Rishy added a coffee shop beside it and a kitchen store upstairs that offered cooking classes. Eventually she added So Chopped Salad Bar & Bistro.

As the remodeling was being done, other vacant spots began to fill. We were looking for the perfect tenant, so we decided to hold a contest called the Pensacola Business Challenge. The winner turned out to be MariCarmen Josephs, a young restaurant manager and chef. She ended up opening Carmen's Lunch Bar, which at the time I write this has just celebrated five years in business.

You can read more about the business challenge in The Titans of Revitalization chapter. Again, it's based on an idea we learned in Asheville and has succeeded far beyond our expectations. In fact, it resulted in several other businesses getting started as well. (The same idea worked well in Janesville, WI.)

As all of this was taking place, the two lots on the south corner became active. Some very innovative people created Al Fresco, which is basically an outdoor dining hotspot with five Airstream food trailers that serve everything from oysters to tacos to chicken & waffles to barbecue. This led to other available spaces being filled with food venues as well. Deshi, a nail salon; Volume ONE, a hair salon; and Fiore of Pensacola, a florist, went into other renovated buildings. A bank from outside the city limits built a brand-new historically themed building on the other corner and renamed itself the Bank of Pensacola. The downtown Saenger Theatre got a major renovation.

Going west on Main Street, Rishy opened the Bodacious Brew Thru drive-thru coffee shop with its early childhood learning playground outside. (You can read more about this in the Focus on Education chapter.) East of the bank on Main Street is a brand-new Holiday Inn Express.

The Downtown Improvement Board, a local merchants association, did a terrific job with bringing programming (and people) downtown. They started a farmers market on Palafox Street that is now held every Saturday. They sponsored all kinds of events downtown like Gallery Night and various festivals, including a variety of holiday activities. They started a First City Lights Festival for the holidays to help drive traffic to bars and restaurants in the off-season. They were also very valuable in getting things started that could then be transferred to others in the community (like a New Year's Eve event and downtown trick or treating). They helped with parking logistics and managed a lot of the critical details for keeping things running smoothly. They were doing the kind of things Jim Clifton had talked about, and it was working. They are terrific ambassadors and have been incredibly engaged in the process.

Palafox Street hadn't quite taken off yet, but it was getting ready. With the work on the park and the stadium gearing up, there seemed to be more positive energy being generated. That energy attracted some social and entertainment hotspots. Joe Abston started Hopjacks and The Tin Cow, two very popular restaurants. Scott Zepp came in with World of Beer.

From there, what had been predicted was coming to life. As energy builds, major investors come in and smaller entrepreneurs will follow. And that's what happened.

Evan and Harry Levin took a vacant Masonic temple on the corner of Palafox and Garden to create the music venue Vinyl Music Hall. (We had learned from Asheville that it's important to have a music place to bring young people downtown.) Then Katie Garrett opened the Old Hickory Whiskey Bar. Other storefronts on Palafox were being filled by retail spots.

Ray Gindroz was right: Every city needs a great intersection. Palafox and Main, which was filled with empty lots and vacant buildings in the late 2000s, is alive and busy today. We're seeing an explosion of the community, and this inter-section is at the center of it all.

Meanwhile, Back at the Waterfront Park...

While all this development was taking place downtown, things were mov-ing along at the Vince J. Whibbs Sr. Community Maritime Park. It was behind schedule, but making progress.

The original plan was that Studer Group® would rent about 20,000 square feet of what would be a 60,000-square-foot office building. We were unsure of who would lease the rest of the space. There had not been a Class-A office built in this area in 30 years. Over the years I've learned that often people cannot visualize a project until they can see it beyond being on paper. Once it started to come together, the demand was a lot greater than originally anticipated, and the project was expanded. What was supposed to be a $12-million, 60,000-square-foot pri-vate office building ended up being a $16-million, 77,000-square-foot building, with a total leasable space of 66,468 square feet. It was originally supposed to be a three-story building, but a fourth story had to be added. To everyone's sur-prise and delight, it filled up quickly. Studer Group ended up needing more than 30,000 square feet. EmCare, a physician staffing company for emergency rooms, took more than 28,000 square feet, and Moore, Hill & Westmoreland, PA, a law firm, leased nearly 5,400 square feet.

This building is a prime example that vertical growth pays for urban sprawl. If an 80,000-square-foot building goes up four stories, it takes up close to the same amount of green space that a single story 20,000-square-foot building would. It pays more than $200,000 in property tax, whereas a one-story building would have created only one-third of that amount in taxes. Some cities insist on restric-tions, but height is good for the tax base and the environment.

On another Community Maritime Park parcel right across the street from the Maritime Place office building, Beck Partners, a real estate insurance company, built a 25,000-square-foot office/retail building. This also added to the tax base.

Wahoos Hit the Field

The Pensacola Blue Wahoos (the Double-A team moved from North Caro-lina), which were named by the community, have an engaged fan base. Though the Wahoos didn't hit the field until April 2012, by early January of that year, Wahoos fans had bought 2,320 season tickets, and outfield signs and scoreboard advertising were sold out.

By the time the Wahoos played their first game in 2012, excitement was at a fever pitch. The Navy's Blue Angels flight team, based in Pensacola, made a flyover timed with the first pitch. The first season drew more than 320,000 fans. Since then, the Blue Wahoos have drawn over 300,000 fans per year to Pensacola.

The Blue Wahoos have created a wonderful fan experience and have won multiple awards over the years. Not only is there a highly engaged fan base, but there are also engaged employees totally dedicated to excellence.

The first year they were eligible, the Wahoos won the coveted Bob Freitas Award for being the best overall franchise among the 30 affiliates at this level. To be eligible, you have to have been a franchise for at least five years, and the award honors franchises at the minor league levels for their overall achievements in community service, fan appreciation, impact in a region, and other aspects. The Blue Wahoos are considered a model franchise in the baseball world, not just in Double-A, but throughout all levels of the sport.

In 2016, the Wahoos also won the Southern League Community Service Award. Giving back to the community is at the heart of our organization.

The programming of downtown worked. In a team effort, many successfully created programs brought lots of people downtown on a regular basis. The park has become a central point for many activities. The stadium hosts the University of West Florida football team, youth football, and many, many other events in addition to Wahoos baseball.

Not only did the park draw people downtown for food, entertainment, and retail, it had proven to be a good ancillary generator of tax revenue. Since the stadium opened, the taxable property value in the Community Redevelopment Agency (CRA) has gone from $675 million to $850 million, an increase of 25.9 percent. The original plan to create a park to revitalize the city to increase tax dollars is working well.

The YMCA Moves Downtown

One night at a baseball game, Harold Dawson Jr., owner of The Dawson Company out of Atlanta, who oversees construction of some of our projects, looked at the empty parcel where the museum was originally supposed to be. He asked me if we had a YMCA in Pensacola. I said yes, it was just north of downtown and very old. He suggested that if we put a new YMCA on that parcel, it would be an important amenity for Pensacola and would be a catalyst for other investments.

So we gave this some thought and decided we should build a new YMCA for Pensacola. This is where philanthropy comes into the story. We are fortunate enough to have some very generous families in our community: the Levin family, the Bear family, and the Switzer family. They all came in between $500,000 and $1 million, and Rishy and I donated the land and contributed $5 million. Between the four families, we were able to get a great start on fundraising for the new YMCA.

Sadly, city politics stopped us from building the Y on the waterfront park parcel. However, the *Pensacola News Journal* had a large building on a block and a half of land for sale that had been on the market for some time. Because of the nature of the newspaper business, they had significantly downsized offices. It was on a 5-acre lot, which we were able to purchase. We gave one acre of the land to build the YMCA. The old *Pensacola News Journal* offices and printing press building were demolished.

The new Y sits one block east of Palafox, just north of Seville Quarter. Having a brand-new YMCA located in the central part of downtown was a big win for the downtown revitalization project. It creates a lot of activity and foot traffic for downtown businesses. The new Y is also considerably more successful, averaging more than twice as many individual visits per day as well as more than twice as many monthly members. Fitness is just one of the advantages. There is also a second wave of benefits. The Y provides many things for the community, like afterschool child care for working families, swimming lessons, and a gathering place for events. When the Y is more successful, it can support more things in the community, and that's a win for everyone.

January 2016 Old Downtown YMCA	January 2017 The Bear Levin Studer Family YMCA
3,480 members	7,987 members
12,904 visits	33,344 visits
430 avg. visits per day	1,075 avg. visits per day

Residential Rounds It Out

With the remaining four acres from the *Pensacola News Journal* property, sights were set on phase four of a vibrant downtown, which was residential. (As a reminder, there were four phases to building a vibrant downtown. They included programming, restaurants/shops/retail, office, and residential.) Southtowne—a new $52-million 258-unit apartment building with retail space—is the largest residential project ever built in Pensacola. This means we now have hundreds of people moving into downtown Pensacola. This will give the downtown business-es the continuity and stability they need if the economy fluctuates.

Across the street from Southtowne, next to the YMCA, there is a new $14.4-million mixed-use building, which will include both office space and retail. Clark Partington, a law firm based in Pensacola, will take the top two floors, and retail will take ground-level space, which is the perfect formula for creating foot traffic downtown.

One of the great things about this is that the infrastructure was already there. This means Pensacola gained over $80 million of investment without having to build new roads and incur other new infrastructure costs. Maximizing existing infrastructure is key to creating a solvent city.

We are now experiencing "street thickening." This happens when your main street gets full, and people want to be close to it, but there's no space so they go to the side streets.

As the YMCA began and Southtowne was announced, another major differ-ence-maker made a large investment on the corner of Palafox and Garden—the historic Brent Block. The Switzer brothers, whose relatives owned the building decades ago, have purchased it and are far along in a $15-million renovation. It includes annex workspace, a niche hotel, retail businesses, and so on.

In reviewing these steps taken in Pensacola—and we'll talk more about them as we move through this book—it has happened one block at a time. What we've learned is if you spread out development too much, you don't get the infill between the areas. So we started on the corner of Palafox and Main and focused our development in that little circle. Then we got a hotel over there, apartment buildings over here, an office building over there.

What happens with circles is that momentum builds and other people start joining in. We focused on building and revitalizing projects in small "circles" that are not too far apart geographically. We would start with one small geographic area and really develop it.

Here's how it works. Once that circle begins to be revitalized, you start working on another circle nearby. Then start developing a third circle. Soon the circles begin to connect and grow together. As more and more businesses move into these areas, you'll start to get infill between them. It's amazing how this works. Before you know it, what once may have been a dying street has become a busy, vibrant one.

A Few More Words About What You'll Learn

The building investments you see are only a fraction of what is really happening in Pensacola. A lot is going on behind the scenes. For example, to support the many new businesses that are springing up, we've taken a lot of action in training and development. This is needed because, while it's important for a community to make it easy to start a new business, it's just as important to help new business owners be successful long term. This is described later in the book.

There is more civic engagement. While the referendum was hard, it got a lot of people thinking about the kind of community they want to have. People are more connected than ever, both to the community and to each other. This sets the stage for future growth and improvement.

To create a vibrant community, the community has got to get the wealth off the sidelines. Early on, there is not a great financial return on investment, so engaging people who have the resources is key. You've got to get people willing to invest in downtown and donate money for projects based on their desire to improve the quality of life for others. The ROI is a better community.

When people who have not been to Pensacola in many years come to Pensacola, they are amazed at the change. The feeling is different. In 2013, Palafox Street was named one of the "Ten Great Streets in America" by the American Planning Association, as part of their national program, Great Places in America. Also, downtown Pensacola was named the 2017 Great Places of Florida People's Choice Winner, following a poll administered by the American Planning Association of Florida. And in 2018 *National Geographic Traveler* magazine named Pensacola in a story celebrating urban renewal, great main streets, and smart development policies.

Food & Wine recently did a feature titled "Wait—Since When Is Pensacola a Thing?" (I loved that they talked about Justine Gudmundson-McCain "returning home" to start her own Palafox Place business, Bluejay's Bakery. This is exactly how we want young people to think of Pensacola.)

While these accolades are nice to have, it's even more important that all the community efforts did in fact create economic growth and community solvency. We talked about this earlier, but it bears repeating. In the last five years, the Community Redevelopment Agency (CRA), went from an assessed property value of $675 million to $850 million, which equates to a 25.9 percent growth. Also, there are projects worth $100 million being built right now that don't even count toward this total. This is the kind of smart growth communities need to shore up their tax base. When making decisions about what to do in your own community, be sure to connect the efforts to economic growth.

First-time visitors react much like we did when we visited Asheville, NC, Charleston, SC, Savannah, GA, or Portland, ME. They think, *We could never do this*. But we found out that they can. There is a blueprint we've put together that is a combination of everyone we have learned from combined with my work over the years in change management and creating high-performing organizations. That blueprint is this book.

Just remember as you read: Relate; don't compare. Every community is different and has unique needs. A stadium might not be right for you. Still, the hope is you will be able to take the ideas and lessons presented here and apply them to your community in a way that makes sense for you. And remember, none of this happens overnight. What you've read about here took place over the span of more than a decade and is still unfolding.

So that's a little of the story. People come downtown and they like it, but what has happened here is much more than that. When we did our polling early on, people talked about wanting land cleared and access to water. But the number-one thing people told us over and over is they wanted a community where their children would have the opportunity to stay. They said we were losing too much talent. They said they understand that their child might move because they *want* to move but they don't want their child to *have* to move because there are no opportunities here.

What we've really seen is that creating a vibrant community is about improving the quality of life for the citizens who live there. And that means that now people can have their children and their grandchildren closer to them. Not a week goes by that someone doesn't come up and tell me that their kids are moving back home because of what's happening now in Pensacola. And that's really the gift.

You'll read in this book how we've created dashboards, you'll read about the quality of life survey, and you'll read about what we've done in response to things we've measured. You'll read about what we did with education and what we did with scholarships. You'll read about successes, about things that went as planned, and about some failures. That's why building a vibrant community is pretty difficult—because no one goes through it undefeated. However, there are probably few things in anyone's life that are as rewarding as building a community where children and grandchildren can stay home and feel like they live in a great community.

We are still on this journey. There are still exciting wins, and there are still disappointments. There are days when one wonders if it's worth it. However, when you see children not leaving, when you see children and grandchildren coming back home, when you see new businesses starting and growing, and when you see an increased focus on education and a better quality of life for all, you will know the answer is *yes*.

Creating a vibrant community is like throwing pebbles in a pond. While each pebble may not make a big splash, each one impacts the water, which creates ripples, which creates more ripples, which changes the pond. All are connected.

So too are many actions in a community. We are all pebbles in the pond of life. Don't underestimate the difference you can and do make.

CHAPTER 3

Getting Started

How does one get started creating a better community? Community members might have some big ideas and plans they are really excited about, but getting started can be a challenge. It's easy to talk about what needs to be done, but how does someone get started?

Back in 1982, I was in a meeting where somebody asked the question, "If you have two frogs on a lily pad and one decides to jump off, how many do you have?" I immediately thought, *Well, two minus one is one.* He said, "No, the answer is two." I remember thinking, *He doesn't even know the answer to this simple math question!* But then he said, "Making a decision and taking action are two different things."

Bingo. That brief moment changed my life.

We can jump off that lily pad into the water and take action. The first thing is to figure out what's holding us back. Why are we stuck?

There are some common obstacles to getting started, and often they are hard to recognize. We all have habits that keep us from changing. For example:

Rationalization. This often happens on an unconscious level. We don't know we are rationalizing and we come up with reasons that make sense to us to not move forward.

One of the biggest rationalizations we hear in working with organizations and communities that have visited Pensacola over the last couple of years is "terminal uniqueness." Basically, people find some way that they are different that gives them a reason not to move forward. When visiting Asheville for ideas, my first thought was, *You have The Grove Park Inn. You have mountains. We don't.*

It's a way of saying, "Your solutions won't work for me." But instead of rationalizing that you're different, communities need to look for similarities. This shift in mindset allows you to identify and implement best practices.

Blame and excuse making. Then there is the tendency to blame and make excuses. People want to blame an elected official for blocking needed change or blame it on the "good ol' boys." The problem is the "good ol' boys" are usually replaced by good new boys (or girls). There will always be some group that people are going to blame for stopping what needs to be done. The challenge is, every time we put one finger out, three are pointing back.

"It didn't work last time." Yes, sometimes the strategies that are going to be implemented have been tried before, but maybe this time you're in a different environment. When things go wrong, it's important that we ask ourselves, *How did this happen?* We're not asking in a blaming way, but history is important. We learn from seeing the context in which events developed, and of course we learn from the mistakes of the past.

For example, people may try to lose weight many times without lasting success, but that doesn't mean they quit trying. Suddenly something happens, whether it's a health scare or they finally hear something in a different way that just clicks and finally they lose weight. Alcoholism and other types of addiction are the same way. Very few people recover on their first attempt, but that doesn't mean they should give up. We have to keep moving forward.

"Someone else will fix it." They won't. We need to stop waiting for others to "fix it." We have to provide our own solutions.

"He wants this only because he's going to make money off the deal." Don't let the fear that someone will make money stop progress. Great cities celebrate citizens' success. Just because someone makes money from a project does not mean they are doing it at the community's expense. In fact, doing well often leads to people investing back into the community. As long as everything is transparent and above board, it's okay that people make money from their investments.

So, getting started means understanding that there are going to be naysayers, there's going to be pushback, and you have to just keep moving ahead. At the root of all of these bad habits is the need for self-protection. What most people are really doing when they resist change in a community is unconsciously protecting their status.

Our excuses show that we are buying into myths. *Someone else is doing it.* Or, *It's too expensive.* Or, *It doesn't work.* Or, *This failed in the past; it will fail again.* In Pensacola, the saying used to be "NFL" meaning "Not For Long." People were buying into the myth that change never lasts. This is not surprising, as people have a history of disappointment. But we need to realize we create our own myths. If we can create our own myths we can create our own success stories, too.

To get unstuck, we must first change the conversation.

In this book we're talking about revitalizing communities. That's not just about building physical infrastructure and creating jobs. It's about changing the culture of a community. It's about making people believe they deserve better than a downtown full of vacant buildings, low graduation rates, and high unemployment rates. That mind shift begins with the language we use.

Peter Block says before we can change a culture we have to stop having the old conversation. On his website, DesignedLearning.com, he writes:

"Whether in a society or an organization, the culture is in many ways defined by the way we talk, the language we use, the nature of the debate and dialogue we engage in… Too often we try to change a culture by focusing on the structure, on the rewards or on the roles and core competencies. These carry a certain logic, but are best preceded by an effort to talk about things that matter in a way that we have not done before. It is the newness of our words to each other that creates the groundwork for changes in practices."[1]

When we start talking about what a great community we already are, why we deserve to get better and better, and how we're going to do it, we start believing it ourselves. Other people start believing it, too. Before long, we've started seeing ourselves as a vibrant community that's well on its way to being even more vibrant. That belief is the first and possibly most important step toward taking action.

When change is forced on you, seize the opportunity to make things better.

Sometimes a community has no choice but to change. An external force makes us start over or reinvent ourselves. An example might be a big company closing down, such as when General Motors closed its facility in Janesville, WI. In her book, *Janesville: An American Story*, Amy Goldstein chronicles Janesville's incredible reinvention after being shaken to its foundation. Goldstein perfectly captures the Janesville community's willingness to embrace change and put all their collective energy into rebuilding their town. Where it might have been easy to spend time gnashing teeth and trying to rebuild the past, many citizens instead focused on imagining a new future and realizing the potential their town still had.

Another example of an external force is at the heart of Pensacola's own story. When Hurricane Ivan came through in 2004, it caused tremendous damage to the community, which we obviously needed to rebuild. That forced us to ask ourselves some hard questions: *Do we simply try to rebuild things the way they were? Or do we try to make them better?* If we just "patch the hole," problems will happen again. This is not real change.

In Pensacola's case, a group of very courageous people got together to look at how to put new roofs on buildings, how to rebuild new roads, and so forth. It was an urgent situation, and people had to move quickly. However, the interesting thing about Pensacola was that the group not only looked at rebuilding the structures, they also asked, *How do we take this event and use it as a catalyst to rebuild the community? How do we make things better than before so that we're more prepared for the future?*

That's the beauty of life: Sometimes what looks like a disaster on the surface can actually be a launching pad for taking things in a new and exciting direction. It all depends on how you look at your circumstances and whether you have the courage to change and the knowledge to make it happen in the right way.

The Psychology of Change

It helps to understand the psychology of change. This knowledge will make our efforts far more effective.

The first thing to know is that people resist change, especially if they are not leading it. It's only human. We resist change in the workplace and we also resist change in the community. Even when we know we need to change, and admit there are big challenges with where we are right now, we can still resist.

So here are some of the things I've learned about leading a change in a community:

First, don't overuse the word "change." It scares people. Instead, share what the change will create. Say, "Let's create a community where young people will want to stay," or, "Let's build a place where people can come downtown and have a good time." Most people want their children and grandchildren to live nearby. Most people want to have fun things they and their friends and family can do nearby. They are less likely to argue when the issue is framed this way.

Second, start out with a realistic goal. There's nothing wrong with setting big goals. James Collins talks about the "big, hairy, audacious goals." I agree to a point, but it's important not to make them *too* big and hairy. If they are too big and hairy, they will scare people.

In the past when I worked with businesses, we always talked about what happens when you set high goals. Of course people don't say to their boss, "Hey, the goal's too high." They might want to say it, but they don't say it. Instead they come up with rational reasons why they can't hit the goal. They'll say things like, "There's too much on our plate. Let's slow down. There are too many priorities. Here's why we can't do it now. Here's why it won't work."

It's no different in a community. People see a goal and get uncomfortable with it (particularly those who might feel they're responsible for that goal).

Yet in business and in communities, a goal can be high if it captures the heart. In healthcare, people will strive to meet high goals because they almost always care about what happens to their patients. Leaders just have to frame what they're asking people to do in a way that connects with that sense of purpose. In communities, goals need to be framed in a way that connects to what citizens care about most.

That means explaining to citizens that we want to create a place where our children can get great educations, where wages are good, and where people are safe. To say we're going to increase our wages by 25 percent might sound too unrealistic. But we can say we are going to make it our goal that our children won't have to leave this town for a job. Even though it's a lofty goal, they'll like it because it connects to their heart.

Get comfortable with the uncomfortable.

The key is to create a vision that people can buy into. Meeting a high goal is going to be a little uncomfortable, but that's okay because they care deeply about it. It shouldn't be so high that it's unreachable, but it should also not aim too low.

Creative tension is what Peter Senge, the author of *The Fifth Discipline*, describes as the space that exists between where people are now and where they want to go. I went to one of his conferences years ago and found it enlightening. What he said about creative tension is that people know where they are, they know where they need to go, and in between is discomfort. Nobody likes to be uncomfortable, particularly a community.

This is why people you might expect to embrace a project won't, particularly when you start uncovering things that might be holding the community back. It could be the community is not where it needs to be with safety. It could be that there are conflicts of interest, and there are some contracts that should have been opened up to others. People who are involved in issues like these may not be too excited about having them uncovered or about ideas to change them.

For example, if your community sets a goal of improving high school graduation rates, there's a possibility that people in the education realm will be hesitant and for a variety of reasons. Certainly, there are many factors that education leaders can't control: the quality of students' home lives, the fact that some of them come to school unprepared, hungry, and so forth. Be sensitive to people taking messages personally. Always remember—and communicate that you realize—that high school graduation rate is *not* a school issue. It is a community issue.

If the goal is to grow the downtown, some people might feel other locations are being left out. They might be worried about losing status or influence or maybe even business. Perhaps they had a monopoly and are worried somebody might come in to compete with them. Or somebody might start worrying, *What happens if you build it and no one comes?*

The important thing is to get comfortable with discomfort. People are going to be uncomfortable. There's no doubt about it. It might be tempting to lower goals in order to lower the creative tension. Don't. It will only create consensus, and very little change comes out of consensus. Everyone ends up unhappy. Seek consent, not consensus.

And keep coming back to why we're doing this in the first place. We're not doing any of this for comfort. We're doing it to create a better community.

A Few More Tips for Dealing With Change

Once efforts to create a vibrant community are underway, it's easy to think the tough part is over and people are now comfortable with the notion of change. No, things are just getting started, and there is a long journey ahead. Change has to be managed continuously. Here are a few more tips for doing it well.

Challenge all assumptions. We might think a project is going to be one thing, but when we start working on it, we'll find that it's likely to change many, many times. This takes humility and flexibility. People need to make sure they are not so married to their ideas that they won't move as needed.

Also, be willing to admit mistakes or to adopt a new position as new information becomes available. This is an issue that people struggle with, especially public officials. Too often they are criticized for changing their opinion or saying they were wrong once new information becomes available. We should commend them for changing their mind, not criticize them for it.

Do not underestimate the importance of trust. We live in a time of declining trust in government and in leaders of all types of organizations. This is why it is so important to build trust with the entire community and to build it early in the process. Here are a few tips:

- Communicate, communicate, communicate. It is impossible to *over*communicate. The more that stakeholders and residents understand the process and what the goal is, the more successful any efforts will be.

- Make sure no one is left out. Any perception that information is shared with only certain groups will kill trust.

- Be respectful of all participants and community members. This includes opponents. Be very, very sure that the tone, messages, and the way they are shared convey complete respect.

- Don't just tell; engage. All stakeholders need to have a way to share their perspective and contribute their ideas and skills.

Practice transparency ALWAYS. Why are people not transparent? Usually it's more of an oversight rather than an intentional choice. People just don't think to communicate what they are doing and why. But especially when making decisions that will have an impact on the lives of our citizens, we must be careful to be transparent in all that we say and do. As Justice Louis D. Brandeis famously said, "Sunlight is said to be the best of disinfectants; electric light the most efficient policeman."

Know that optimism and skepticism are both contagious. One of the most important jobs of a community change agent is to build optimism, keep the momentum going, and squelch skepticism. A few tips:

- Generate small wins. This builds people's confidence and generates optimism. When people see that success has happened, they believe it can happen again.

- Pepper the team with optimistic people. The more optimists on your team the better.

- Don't let skeptics and naysayers get a foothold. Some people will never be satisfied with anything. Don't let them drain your own energy and enthusiasm, or, worse, detract from the positive feelings being cultivated in the community.

- Learn from mistakes. When things go wrong, focus people on the teachable moments. Positive results are almost always born from even the worst experience. Don't allow those around you to get mired in what went wrong. Instead, redirect them to what good might come from what has happened or to what can be learned from what went wrong.

- Say thank you loudly, publicly, and often. Gratitude is an extremely powerful force. When people know they are appreciated, it raises their energy. They like you more and will be willing to work even harder to meet your goals.

Once starting on the journey toward creating a vibrant community, the victories, both large and small, will keep the team going. The energy they generate will hopefully overpower the discomfort of change and help to keep the momentum going. But to ensure that happens, it's necessary to be able to work productively with all of the different types of people one might encounter along the way…and that's what the next chapter is about.

CHAPTER 4

Dealing With Personality Types and Setbacks

Revitalizing a community is not an easy task. Determining the right path and what will work for a community requires a lot of complex decision making and critical thinking. Getting groups to agree on priorities and how best to execute them will be difficult. Things will likely not go smoothly, at least not all the time.

Many people on the journey will be absolutely wonderful and help move the goals of the community forward. Yet there are others who won't help and perhaps a few who will actively work against the plans and actions.

This is true in all areas of life. Building a vibrant community is no exception. I've visited and spoken to many types of communities. Reflecting on the types of people who get involved in communities early on and stay involved has been a learning experience.

If moving a community forward is even being discussed, that means somebody is concerned about it not growing, or falling behind, or even experiencing a disaster or failure. Sometimes a community has experienced a major loss. For example, Janesville, WI, lost the General Motors plant (and what a wake-up call that was). Other times an external force like a hurricane or a tornado makes it obvious that something has to be done. Sometimes it's simply about taking a good community and making it better.

Different Types of People

People generally fall into one of the following four categories:

1. The first type of person will grab onto the idea because they feel it's the right thing to do. Support these people. Thank them. Keep them in the loop because they will be vital in pushing it forward.

2. The second type of person likes the idea and has identified the WIIFM (What's In It For Me). Be sure to keep the benefits in front of these people at all times!

3. The third type of person may not be personally invested in the merit of the idea, but can clearly see how it could benefit them. Don't take their motive personally. What's important is to keep this group supportive.

4. Finally, the fourth type of person will be against virtually everything. Don't spend precious time and energy worrying about these people. Be respectful, but don't be fooled into thinking that more information or more inclusion will make a difference.

Two of the groups—the "very much for" group and the "very much against" group—will come out early and feel very strongly about their convictions. To move a project that depends on a lot of community support, it is vital to keep that "very much for" group with you while you listen to, at times adjust to the input from, and educate the people in the middle two groups.

Four Types of People

When working to move a community forward, there are usually four types of people working for the changes, against the changes, or somewhere in between. It's important to understand and have a strategy for all four categories. To help illustrate how the four categories impact change in your community, they are described below in terms of what we saw with the Community Maritime Park Project in Pensacola.

The first type. This is the type of person who quickly has a connection to the project and sees how the community will benefit. It connects with their heart and mind. This group can be very diverse. The Community Maritime Park Project strongly attracted this type of person.

For example, it attracted young adults who saw the project as one that would create a more fun place to live and work. They had been to other communities and asked, "Why not? Why can't Pensacola be like some of the other exciting places where we have visited or gone to school?"

The minority population saw the park as something that could create jobs and a more level playing field. This was especially true when we created the Covenant for the Community. (This is explained in the Think Inclusion chapter and is reprinted in Appendix A.) It guaranteed a certain percentage of the jobs involved in this project would go to local residents. (Studer Properties has continued this covenant with all our projects.)

Also, there was a group of people whose children had moved away because of lack of opportunity who were early supporters of the Community Maritime Park Project. They had heard from their children that there just was not enough economic incentive to stay in Pensacola.

Another group was made up of newer residents. They came from communities in which they had seen success with what was being recommended and wanted the same thing in Pensacola.

There was also a group who was just excited about progress. They believed the project would make our community better and move things forward.

Type 1 consists of people who may not know each other well to start with. The neat thing is that their common goal helps create relationships and a sense of ownership regarding the importance each person makes. Everyone has an important voice and they are all connected by their passion for making the community better.

The second type. In Pensacola, this group was similar to the first group, except not as zealous. They had some reservations. However, the more they learned, and the more they saw that a vibrant community would create more opportunity for themselves and their companies, the more supportive they became. This group leaned toward supporting the project after more encouragement and explanation as to how it would work. It is very common for Type 2s to become more supportive as the "What's In It For Me" dots are connected.

The third type. While the second group was leaning toward supporting the Community Maritime Park, the third group was leaning toward not supporting it. This position may have come from the fact that they had been let down previously with unfulfilled promises. In addition, the opposition (Type 4) was working hard on this group with misinformation and scare tactics.

The fourth type. Finally, this group seems to gain their purpose by being against virtually everything. There are times when being against a project makes great sense and is healthy. What sets this group apart from that is they tend to fight everything and they tend to be really good at it. This resistance is not new behavior; they likely have done this for much of their lives.

Type 4 people often don't bring forward their own plans, but are quick to say no to others. There was a group diametrically opposed to the Community Maritime Park Project. This opposing group was asked for the name of an urban planner we could bring in to give us solid advice on how to move the city forward. They supplied a name and we brought the urban planner in. When they didn't agree with his recommendations, they basically said, "Well, that's because the other side paid for him." You will not win with this group.

Tips for Building Relationships and Leveraging Support with Each of the Four Groups

Type 1

Take time to get to know these people. They are a diverse group and they often don't know you or each other that well. Find out their *what* (what drives them, what they feel passionate about) and why they feel as they do. They want to have an impact. Remember, this group often becomes the first line of volunteers. From serving on small teams to walking the neighborhoods, these people want to have a role. This is great, for they are needed; after all, it is easier to get a no than a yes. Thank them for their support and keep them recognized and appreciated. Their greatest reward is to see the project work.

Leaders of these efforts bear a great responsibility to deliver to the best of their ability the promised outcome. The reason people are reluctant to get on board early is they have done so in the past and been let down. It is very gratifying today to see these people who in 2004, 2005, and 2006 spent so much time on the Community Maritime Park Project feel good about their work in getting the referendum passed.

Type 2

This group leans in a positive direction; however they are not ready to go all in. This could be true for a number of reasons: past disappointments, personality issues with some of the strong supporters, worries that they will be shut out from gaining new work (for they feel contract decisions are a done deal), and so on. The reasons will vary widely.

The good news is many in the group are leaning toward being supportive, but they need more reasons why. Connecting the dots on the short- and long-term gains is critical. Short-term gains might be the number of construction jobs that become available. Longer-term gains might include attracting more investments; more people staying in town and more moving back or to the community for the first time; an increased tax base for schools, safety, and infrastructure; as well as an overall better quality of life.

Connecting these dots is important for each of the first three groups, but it is critical for this group. The more they can connect to the benefits for others and for themselves the more they will move to supporting the project. At times they will become as strong in support as those who are Type 1.

Type 3

Remember, while it's important to focus most of the energy on those first two groups, do not ignore Type 3. While they lean against the project—and the majority may stay that way—getting some of this group to move toward support can make the difference between a go and a no-go. Provide them with the facts and realize that the more you can connect to how they will benefit personally, the more likely it is they will become supporters.

Don't judge them. Like Type 2s, it could be they have been promised things in the past that did not happen. Maybe they just feel things are being said to get their support, and once the project starts those commitments of a fair playing field will be forgotten.

Be attentive to this group for they can make a difference; however, do not have unrealistic expectations. The good news is if they lean against the project and it does go forward anyway, they will be glad. They do want what is best for the community; they just had issues at the time that prevented them from being supportive.

In Pensacola, 7,000 people voted against the Community Maritime Park Project. It is a very common occurrence for one of them to come up to me and tell me they voted no and they were wrong and are glad they were. While this group may not be supportive at first, if promises are kept, many in this group will move to Type 1 or 2 in the future.

Type 4

Sadly, what we've learned is that this group is often the most verbal one. They're the people who are really going to fight change. They require a lot more time and sometimes a lot more money to even consider giving a yes. As a state senator told me one time at a conference, "It's much easier to get a no than a yes."

My experience is most people fall into one of three mindsets. Given the same set of circumstances, they will come up with three very different "takes" on what happened. Mindset 1 is "win-win." These people find a way for both sides to benefit. People with Mindset 2 can't believe there is such a thing as a win-win. They believe there must be a winner and a loser. And then there's Mindset 3: the "lose-lose" mindset. When you talk to these people, they're just excited that the other side lost—even though they also lost and so did the entire community. These people fall into the Type 4 group.

We spent a lot of time and a lot of energy trying to convince the "unconvince-able." And that's why I say the best strategy for this group is to be careful not to do that. It is necessary, however, to address them sometimes. Early on during the referendum we thought we would just stay silent when things were said that were incorrect or misleading. However, we eventually learned we had to speak up on some things.

We were really fortunate to have a supporter named Jeff DeWeese who was willing to go to all meetings. When something came up he knew was not accurate, he would bring it up and try to correct it. We eventually took out a newspaper ad that showed the myths versus the facts. We found that was a good way to get correct information in front of people.

Limit the precious time and energy you spend worrying about these people. This learning is very much in hindsight for me. In an altruistic manner, we just kept thinking more information and more discussion would make a difference. It does not. What it does do is keep one from spending time with those in Types 1, 2, and even, as time permits, Type 3.

Consent Versus Consensus

You win some and you lose some. For sure no one goes undefeated. In Pensacola we were excited because we thought we had something the whole community could get behind—but we finally figured out that the whole community will never be behind anything.

For every community project, the break out will be different. When the Community Maritime Park Project vote was taking place, we had an even split to start with from each category. This means about 25 percent of the community was Type 1. They came to meetings, wore buttons, and thought it was great. They were zealots. About 25 percent of the community was Type 2—not certain, but leaning toward a yes. About 25 percent was Type 3—pretty skeptical, but not a hard no. And about 25 percent was Type 4 and were totally against it. They key is to keep the first two groups solidly with you and try to swing as many as you can from Type 3. Don't expect a lot, but sometimes you don't need a lot.

Ellis Bullock, a public relations and marketing guru, often reminded me of the minimum number of votes we needed to get the project through. He said to just focus on the votes you need to swing and let the rest go. Trying to convince the entire group was likely a waste of our time. We'd be better off spending our time cementing relationships with people who would ultimately support us.

That was a hard lesson to learn, because most people are pleasers by nature and really want to make everyone happy, but it just won't happen. Be polite and stay on the high ground, but don't spend a ton of time on this last quadrant. Spend the time on the other three quadrants.

As you can see, creating change is very rarely smooth sailing. People have different motives, different personalities, and different priorities. That means there will always be disagreements and resistance. Only by expecting these challenges and having a strategy for dealing with them can progress be made.

Remember in the last chapter we talked about creative tension? When working with other people, there is going to be tension, because people are going to be uncomfortable. There's nothing wrong with tension, but the key is not to let it lower the vision or lower the goal. Creating an educated and engaged community is never a smooth path. The only thing that can be done is to continue improving your skillset and communication and keep building on that critical mass.

Dealing with Pushback and Differing Opinions

It's important to know why people oppose things. For our project, there were people who opposed it simply because they didn't think it would be successful. Some people liked all grass. Others wanted lots of buildings. Still others called the project a giveaway. Knowing why certain people opposed it helped tremendously in dealing with them on an individual level.

Of course, we don't always get our way, and people aren't always going to like us. We need to be prepared for this. And that's okay. Anyone who *everyone* likes and agrees with is likely not accomplishing very much.

Expect a lot of defeats and personal rejections along the way.

As we were going through the referendum on the Community Maritime Park Project, my wife, Rishy, and I would get some ugly mail anonymously sent to our house. One time a person named Charlie walked up to me at the city council meeting, looked straight at me, took his wallet out of his back pocket, and put it in his front pocket. The message was that I was a pickpocket. Words like "carpet-bagger" got thrown around, and it was pretty uncomfortable.

I remember Rishy and me giving each other one of those, *Why are we involved in this?* looks. I'm sure other people were feeling the same way. We were having to constantly remind ourselves why we were doing this. We had to say, "We're not doing it for comfort. We're doing it to create a better community."

Anytime a community is going through change, there will be defeat and rejection. How setbacks are managed is everything. A few tips for dealing with setbacks:

- Don't take things personally, even though the attacks can get personal. People sometimes let their emotions get the best of them.

- Stay positive. People notice. This is especially important for leaders as they often set the tone for the mood of the group.

- Focus on the end result. Giving oxygen to silly things or minor distractions creates exhaustion. This is where leaders start to fall apart. Frustration, anger, and exhaustion are all really expensive fuel!

- Keep it in perspective. Remember that there is more than this one failed project. The community is bigger than the one referendum that didn't pass.

- Learn to see setbacks as catalysts for growth and learning experiences. Anyone who *never* fails isn't challenging the status quo enough. What can be learned from this experience? What might be done better next time?

- Talk openly about defeats and rejections. Don't hide them. People respect honesty and appreciate vulnerability.

- Give detractors a chance to join the group in a graceful way and be willing to stay with the group, even when there's a disagreement.

- Fail fast. Even the most successful people are going to fail, so move past it quickly. Don't dwell on the negative, but throw yourself wholeheartedly into the next project.

Finally, here are a few big lessons we learned from working with people on community projects:

- Be careful of accepting generalizations. People say things like "a lot," "everyone," and "some," etc. to describe things. Ask people to be specific.

- Make people speak for themselves. If someone says, "people are saying," or, "good old boys," ask who they are talking about. Then ask, "Well, how do *you* feel about it?"

- Always encourage very specific feedback.

- Don't carry someone's message to another person. Help them go directly to the person and even help them arrange a meeting if needed.

- Be very cautious about getting into social media comments. It can burn lots of time and be a huge distraction. The negative attackers want to get a reaction. Don't bite.

- It's a marathon. There will be peaks and valleys. There will be periods of energy and there will also be calmer times. If we don't pace things, we wear out ourselves and our team members.

- We have an obligation to speak up with the truth. It's part of creating an educated, engaged community. When incorrect statements come up, do politely provide the correct information.

This chapter has shared some universal truths about dealing with people and setbacks. Chances are they apply to what you're experiencing, at least in some capacity. But your path to becoming vibrant won't be exactly like Pensacola's. Every community has different challenges and needs different solutions. And that's the subject of the next chapter: how to make sure the journey of change is the best one possible for your unique community.

CHAPTER 5

Creating a Tailored Approach for Your City

When a community is ready to start making serious changes, it might be tempting to just jump in and start doing something because of the actions taken by another community. One might think, *Well, the next county over did this and it worked.* Be careful. Resist this temptation. Every community is different and has different needs. That's why it's important to use objective measurements up front to get an accurate picture of what needs to be done.

When visiting a doctor, they don't give you a treatment plan before performing an examination and providing a diagnosis. Be careful not to jump into the treatment of a problem too soon. We can be too quick to implement an idea because we are eager to achieve results quickly. We are often quick to jump on a bandwagon.

Of course, this problem is not limited to community-building. There is a great deal of pressure to perform faster and better everywhere in our society. Not only do we want to fix a problem, we want to accomplish it in record time. Unfortunately, rushing can set us up for failure down the road. Without a proper diagnosis, we cannot effectively treat the problems we face or sustain results.

The issues and opportunities are not the same for every community. Replicating other ideas without making sure they make long-term sense for your community can result in costly mistakes.

Get educated before making a diagnosis.

"The wise man is one who knows what he does not know."
—Lao Tzu

The world is changing rapidly. New approaches and possibilities are being developed every day, and it's important to look at all of them. The real question is: *What's a tailored approach for* our *community?* The answer may come from outside your community, and it may be something that has never been considered.

Not only can communities not be expected to have the answers, they may not even have a good handle on what the issues are. That's why when we were starting to revitalize Pensacola, we did a lot of research up front and sought out experts.

How did we prepare? We read books. We consulted experts. We brought in urban planners and other big thinkers for a community lecture series and workshops. The key is to balance research because too much planning and not enough action can create a problem.

Jim Clifton, chairman and CEO of Gallup, taught us a lot about what creates thriving communities. From him we learned a lot about supporting the right kinds of companies, helping start-ups get off the ground, and orchestrating all the factors that create vibrant downtowns. Ray Gindroz from Urban Design Associates in Pittsburgh not only helped us educate people and get community input, he drilled down into some of the details of city development. For example, he taught us about the importance of having a great intersection and maximizing traffic flow.

The great thing about seeking out these types of outside experts is they have no agenda and can be totally objective. They have no dog in the hunt. Having research and data helps substantiate decision-making. Also, having an outside voice to cite can often help settle disagreements.

No doubt about it, this is tricky stuff. It's not easy. If it were easy, we'd all do it, and every community would be vibrant right now. They wouldn't have vacant stores, closed strip malls, vacant parcels of land, and flat taxes. Young people wouldn't be leaving the community. People who would love to move back home would be able to do so, because there would be plenty of jobs.

Once people get educated on the factors that go into creating a vibrant community, they at least begin to know what they don't know. They'll have a starting point for tackling the community's challenges in a measured and thoughtful way. And they'll be ready to move to the diagnosis phase and learn what's really holding the community back.

Why Proper Diagnosis Is So Important

There are many reasons to diagnose where the community is. First, it helps ensure you are treating the right problems. This happens more often than one might expect. Solutions can be pretty costly, and most communities can't afford to focus on the wrong things.

Diagnosis helps identify front-burner issues. It's important to focus on them rather than getting distracted by secondary issues—or focusing on what is easiest to fix. It also prevents people from pushing through certain projects for self-serving reasons and ensures that the loudest voices aren't driving everything.

The idea is to figure out what works for *your* community. Just because an approach works for one community doesn't mean it will work for all communities.

Diagnosis also creates specificity, which gets people focused and generates a sense of urgency. Everyone might know the economy is struggling or have a vague sense that there's a feeling of gloom and hopelessness in the air. But until they know why—what's at the root of the depressed economy or negative culture—they don't know what they can do to fix it. So they do nothing. Once there's a diagnosis, there's naturally a sense of urgency to fix it.

Diagnosis allows for ownership. Knowing what needs improvement—say, poverty levels or high school graduation rates—means people have something to rally around. Solving that problem becomes a goal they can own. Then, it's up to leaders to bring this message to citizens so they can take action and begin fixing it.

But before a community can get a diagnosis rolling, they need to have a team in place.

Building Out a Team

This is where citizen-powered change really begins. Everyone with a leadership role in revitalizing a community needs a lot of help and support. The first step is to identify key players in the community and get clear on their roles.

Choose residents who have skin in the game. Be sure to look to those people Jim Clifton calls "tribal leaders." These are the people who may not have a formal position but are seen as leadership in a community: attorneys, architects, PR people, accountants, journalists and reporters, religious and civic leaders, etc.

As Clifton writes in his book *The Coming Jobs War*, "They know the people to talk to, they know the levers to pull, and they get things done. When they act together, they can accomplish things that *no one* else can."[1]

These folks are committed to the long-term health of the community. They provide the human capital that makes projects sustainable, and you will likely need their expertise. Plus, they want the community to grow and thrive.

Every city, whether it's small, mid-sized, or large, has this group. They just have to be identified, aligned, and galvanized. It's so important to have business leaders on the team as they are the catalyst for change in many cases. It's important to have people who can identify opportunity.

Every team also needs a quarterback. To transform things, having someone who can move the ball down the field is a must. Ideally this person will be able to work the channels, pull groups together, and leverage networks.

Once the players are identified, define their roles. What does this group really need to do for the project? Make sure they know exactly what they need to do and give them the resources they need to do it. Nurture them. Communicate with them. Reward and recognize them often, because without their ongoing commitment, it's impossible to create a vibrant community.

Remember, these people are being asked to make far more than a financial commitment. Revitalizing a community is hard and often thankless work. It can be physically and emotionally exhausting. They have to know that leadership truly cares about the greater mission and also about them as individuals.

Any successful effort will need a good core group that will take the time and make the effort to continuously get the message out that the projects they're advocating for are good for the community. Create an army of citizens who understand and buy into the vision. This team of smart and dedicated leaders are the generals who lead that army into the "battle" that's the tough, frontline work of building a vibrant community.

Benchmarking Other Cities

In improving a community, as in so many other areas of life, there is no need to reinvent the wheel. Know what right looks like, and when you find it in another community, harvest their best practices. This is an efficient and cost-effective way to approach the journey. What have other communities done that can be replicated? What is their "secret sauce" or recipe?

Today there are great websites that regularly point out what others are doing. Also, as you see things, take time to ask. When Mort O'Sullivan was in Charleston in the mid-2000s, he stopped in to Mayor Riley's office and asked what they had done to recreate Charleston. Mayor Riley was happy to help. This was our experience with other cities; they are usually happy to help other communities.

When we were starting to revitalize Pensacola, we took a trip to Asheville, NC, which has a thriving downtown, and learned how they did it. We talked a little bit about this in The Pensacola Story chapter. At first we thought, *We could never do this!* They reminded us where they started and how long it took them to get to this point, and then they took us through their process. By breaking their journey into small, incremental steps, they were able to help us get started. We ended up putting many of their ideas into practice. Sure, there are differences between one community and another, but there are also commonalities. Relate; don't compare.

There were a few other cities we benchmarked as well: Charleston, SC, Greenville, SC, Savannah, GA, Beloit, WI, and Portland, ME. These cities have been so helpful to Pensacola on our journey. Cities that have had some success with revitalization are often more than willing to help. They are excited to share what they have learned, and they can help prevent costly mistakes.

Now it's time to move on to the specifics of measurement.

Metrics and Dashboards: What Gets Measured Increases Chances of Improvement

Any great organization takes careful measurements of their key performance indicators and keeps track of them on a dashboard. Even if they don't call it a dashboard, good organizations have an organized way to see at a glance how they're performing in key areas.

The idea is to show all the crucial metrics together in a "big picture" that tracks progress on the organization's goals. The dashboard shows the bright spots as well as what needs work.

From my many years of work in healthcare, I know how important it is for complex organizations to keep the metrics in front of decision-makers (especially the CEO) at all times. There's just no other way to make smart decisions about how best to use their resources to meet their goals.

Communities are no different. They need objective metrics to know how healthy they are, to identify areas that need improvement, and to gauge progress over time. They also need to be able to see the metrics all together and updated as soon as new information becomes available.

Think of this as the dashboard of a car that shows you how you're doing on gas, oil, engine performance, temperature, and so forth. It's a way to constantly be asking, *How is our community doing on areas that are important to us? Wages? Crime? Education? High school dropout rate?*

The importance of having a dashboard became apparent to me early on in the journey to creating a vibrant Pensacola when somebody brought me reports that were done in other cities. I got these large glossy books (usually created by publicly funded organizations). For me, I found that these kinds of dashboards were just too large and overwhelming. It's possible to compile reports that measure so many things that nothing really gets accomplished. When people can't see where to focus, the report becomes meaningless. That's why it's better to keep dashboards simple and manageable. Be careful not to spin the data. This is not a public relations campaign. It is an important measuring stick of what is good and what needs to get better.

Studer Community Institute worked with the University of West Florida Office of Economic Development and Engagement to develop our dashboard (please see Appendix B). It contains 17 metrics that provide a snapshot of Pensacola's growth and its educational, economic, and social well-being. We keep it posted on our website at www.studeri.org and update it as often as possible.

The metrics represent the Pensacola Metropolitan Statistical Area (MSA) for Escambia and Santa Rosa counties. The goal is to encourage all who impact these quality-of-life aspects to help move these local outcomes to be the best in the state of Florida.

In Pensacola, we also invested in a really good quality of life survey. It yielded yet another set of metrics. We wanted to measure hard facts, sure, but we also wanted to know how people were feeling. The idea was to hear from everybody, not just a few individuals reporting on what they *think* people want.

The first Pensacola Quality of Life Survey was completed in 2007. It was done by Mason-Dixon Polling & Research located in Washington, DC, to conduct a survey of local registered voters. The key is to use the same survey company and questions each year. This helps in year-to-year comparisons.

The survey shows how people are feeling about various aspects of life in Pensacola and Escambia County, including employment opportunities, economic growth, education, confidence in local government, and the environment. To see a copy of the 2017 Quality of Life Survey results, please visit www.pensacolayp.com.

Together, the Pensacola Metro Dashboard and the Mason-Dixon Quality of Life Survey provide area residents with a clear picture of what is going well in our community and where opportunities for improvement exist.

Keep this dashboard in front of everyone at all times. Update it yearly and communicate results.

Every city's dashboard will be different. But it's important to have one and here's why.

Benefits of a Community Dashboard

There are many good reasons to create a dashboard. Here are a few of them:

A dashboard helps make decisions on facts, not opinions. This is probably the most important reason. Few communities can afford to make wrong or shortsighted decisions on how to spend taxpayer dollars or make other changes that affect their citizens' quality of life. Decisions need to be based on hard numbers rather than guesses or personal preferences.

It shows the bright spots. Chip Heath and Dan Heath, coauthors of *Switch*, say that one of the keys to change is focusing on bright spots of performance. Focusing on success helps create more of it.

It forces attention on the most pressing problems. Everyone's problems are different. For example, Pensacola's dashboard shows we have a low high school graduation rate, and that's why one of our big focuses is education. Janesville, WI, has a 93 percent graduation rate. Instead of focusing on fixing education, they might focus on the vacant properties downtown or on some other pressing problem from their dashboard.

It helps in connecting seemingly unconnected dots. In Pensacola, we noticed that our metrics for kindergarten readiness and metrics for high school graduation in Escambia County were identical. Both were at 66 percent. Is there a connection? Could it be a coincidence? So we did research and started connecting dots we had not noticed before. This led us to focus on early brain development and become an Early Learning City. Without the dashboard, we may not have made the connection. The low graduation rate was really a symptom of children not being ready for kindergarten. By focusing on children from birth to three years old, we were able to significantly impact kindergarten readiness, which significantly impacted our graduation rates.

It keeps one from making excuses. If there is a low-performing high school and it happens to be in a poor area, it can be tempting to blame that on poverty. But if the dashboard shows another high school in a similar geographic area has the same poverty level, yet is performing well, you'll know there's some other problem (and the good news: there's a solution).

It creates comparison opportunities with other communities. You can consult and collaborate with them to see how they solved their challenges.

A Few Insights Gained by Dashboards

As with the rest of our journey, there was a lot we didn't know when we set out to create our dashboard. Some things that have happened have not been surprising but others have been. Here are a few of the lessons along the way:

Expect pushback. People have a lot of fear of measurement. As mentioned earlier, we did the quality of life survey because we thought it was vitally important to know how the community feels. Not everyone welcomed this survey. It's been interesting to see that when I talk to communities I find there is a certain amount of fear around the notion of measurement. Truly, this is not unusual.

When I was working with organizations and recommended they measure things like employee engagement, there was always a little bit of pushback. Sometimes it's a money issue, but sometimes it's fear. People don't want to hear news that they feel is going to be bad. Ironically, when organizations do an employee engagement survey, after it's over, they're usually pretty happy they did it. First of all, the results are usually a little better than they expected. Second, it really points out what they need to work on, and leaders know having knowledge is a good thing.

Challenge generalities. I've been at city council meetings and had people walk up and announce how "everyone" feels about an issue. They say it like they are representing 350,000 people. Of course, this is probably not the case. Elected officials sometimes say, "My constituency is really upset about this." One time someone told me they had gotten a lot of emails on an issue. It kind of sounded like this person was up all night combing through emails. But when I asked, "Well, how many did you get?" it turned out the answer was less than three.

The point is that when someone says "a lot of people" or "my constituency" most of us don't think to challenge them. We should. Unchallenged generalities are harmful to a community.

Keep dashboards as simple as possible. As I mentioned before, it's possible to create a dashboard that measures so many things that nothing ever gets accomplished. People are overwhelmed and paralyzed. Keep the metrics to a minimum and people are more likely to act on them because it feels doable.

Once the dashboard is created, keep it updated and in front of the whole community. In Pensacola we work with the local paper and use video to present updates to residents on a regular basis. It's important to keep the metrics very, very transparent. Even if a report is not so great, share it openly.

Don't spend a lot of marketing dollars on a glossy community report. Smart people can go to a website and read the data. There's no reason to spend a lot of money this way, especially taxpayer dollars. The media can be a great partner in helping to share dashboard metrics so be sure to cultivate a good relationship with them.

Once the dashboard is created and the community can see and understand the metrics, solutions come about. *Remember that solutions belong to the entire community.* If there's a safety issue, hopefully public officials will take the lead.

But if the problem is in an economic development area, we can't rely on just one group to "fix it." *Everyone* is responsible for creating jobs in their community.

If we want to create a thriving community, we have to share that message with citizens and we have to make it loud and clear. But we will never, ever move people to action with raw metrics alone. We have to bring some emotion to the discussion. We have to connect to their heart and make people see what's in it for them before they will agree to change. And that's what we'll focus on in the next chapter.

CHAPTER 6

Best Odds for Success

When seeking change, creating momentum and gaining critical mass are vital. Shifting community habits and behaviors is tough and not for the faint of heart. Don't think that once people see objective data, changes will follow. It's just a step in the process.

Providing data to people won't automatically change thinking or behavior. Providing proof that something needs to happen and giving people the facts and figures won't always move them to act. If it did, no one would have heart disease. We would all eat right and exercise and not smoke. But what if the doctor said, *If you don't stop smoking and lose 50 pounds, you won't make it to your daughter's wedding?* That's different, because it connects directly to something people care about.

John Kotter talks extensively about engaging the heart and appealing to emotions to motivate change. Here's what his article in the *Ivey Business Journal* had to say:

"In *The Heart of Change: Real-Life Stories of How People Change Their Organizations* (Harvard Business School Press, 2002), John Kotter and Dan Cohen describe three important limitations of using only facts or analysis to motivate people to change. First, analysis is not needed to find the big truths in most cases. It often doesn't take a detailed financial analysis to determine that the organization is in dire straits. Second, in a turbulent, fast-paced world, analytical tools are often limited due to the frequent changes in parameters and assumptions.

Third, analysis, however astute, rarely motivates people in a big way. Presenting facts alone will inspire few organizational citizens to commit to specific, challenging goals."[1]

Years ago, I was involved in a school referendum. The school district hadn't passed a referendum in years and they had used every fact-based approach they possibly could think of. They showed pictures of the roofs that needed to be fixed and talked about how the tax dollars were still lower than other communities' tax dollars. None of it was working. We were very fortunate to have the support of a person who was in the advertising world and they ran some ads that showed grandparents sitting by a fireplace with grandchildren playing. The ad said, "Somebody paid for our education. Shouldn't we pay for theirs?" That actually moved the needle on the referendum. It spoke to the people's hearts.

The bottom line is that work has to be done to figure out the *why*—meaning why people get up in the morning and go to work and keep on living—and once that is identified, then figure out how to connect it to the message. Our gut instinct is to present the facts, but according to research, most people make a decision with their heart. In fact, around 80 percent of decisions are made with the heart versus 20 percent with the mind. Connect the data to something they care about and then they will act. People make decisions more on heart than on data.

The Burning Platform

To connect to the heart strings, a burning platform is important. *Burning platform* is a popular change management term. It's based on the true story of a tragedy that happened on an oil production platform in the North Sea. Essentially, people had to choose to jump 15 stories and probably die or stay on the burning oil rig and face certain death. So change management folks now use the burning platform metaphor to illustrate that people have to feel a direct personal threat before they will stop being complacent and start to move forward.

In Pensacola, we found two burning platforms. One of them was something you don't wish on anybody. In September of 2004, Hurricane Ivan came through and caused horrendous damage to northwest Florida. We thought some out-of-the-area money would be coming, but a tsunami hit Indonesia around the same time and much of that money went there. While we did get some government money, much of the rebuilding of the community was left to the citizens of Pensacola.

The burning platform was pretty evident at first: how to get homes rebuilt, how to get roads rebuilt, and how to get bridges rebuilt. In fact it was more than that. It was how to get a community rebuilt. And while you can never replace lives lost, can you make that community even better than it was? So we had no choice about one of the burning platforms. But then we found an even better burning platform, one that would impact Pensacola long term.

In polling we found that people had come to the realization that the community was losing too much talent. They realized job growth and more diverse opportunities were needed—and urgently. People knew the community was hurting economically. Research showed a vibrant downtown would attract companies and talent. There was evidence to show that if we took certain steps to create a vibrant downtown, jobs would come.

However, we just could not get momentum behind the change until we got our second burning platform: How can we keep the talent here at home and attract talent back that left? What can we do to keep our children and our grandchildren from leaving? Once we realized this was the burning platform, we could move on to the second step of creating the critical mass that would allow real momentum to build up.

As John Kotter writes, in order to get a group to critical mass, it's important to engage them emotionally. Remember, it is said that 80 percent of decision-making happens in the heart. The heart was the key driver.[2]

Until we started talking about the problem in terms of "our children are leaving," we couldn't get enough people behind the necessary change. Once they understood that no jobs meant children had no place to work so they *had* to move away, that motivated them to act. *The longer we wait, the more children leave.*

That was our burning platform. That was our *why.* That was the goal: to take action to create a better city for our children and to bring people back home.

When change doesn't work, the reason is often that not enough was done to create that burning platform. So what is the burning platform? It could be low graduation rates, it could be wage gap issues, it could be not having the right infrastructure, it could be not having enough jobs. The key is for each community to identify their burning platform.

Sometimes we have to do a better job of explaining the *whys* behind our proposed change in a way that will be meaningful to citizens. Different people have different *whys*, so the *whys* have to be tailored to each group. We have to narrate the WIIFM (What's In It For Me) in terms that will resonate with them. For example:

Group	What's In It For Me?
Small Business Community	More Revenue
Minorities	More Opportunities to Level the Playing Field
Parents	Better Life for Children and Grandchildren
Healthcare Organizations	Good Payer Mix and More Talent
Religious Organizations	More Support for Charities
Politicians	Happy, Thriving Constituency
Citizens	More Job Opportunities/ Safer Communities
Children	Human Potential Maximized

Sequencing

How do you decide where to start? Which steps need to happen first? It's like putting a puzzle together. It's crucial to roll things out in the right order and not try to do everything at once. However, do not expect perfection. Also, be careful not to get too far ahead of the community. Sometimes those coordinating the project are too close to it. They feel the community is also as aware of the project. Be careful not to overestimate how well people understand the actions being taken in the community. Take time to listen to lots of people. Polling can help you figure out how the community thinks and feels.

Keep the scope small and doable.

Cities tend to want to run a marathon all at once. It's great that people have this level of passion but it's not a good idea to try to do too much at one time. It's too easy to get overwhelmed when doing it that way. A measured, deliberate approach is better.

When I was working at Baptist Hospital, one of the things we did to improve post-hospital stay recovery was make post-visit phone calls. For those who don't know, these are the calls made by healthcare personnel after a patient has been discharged. The healthcare professional checks in, makes sure the patient understands and is following discharge instructions, is taking medications properly, asks if they have any questions, and so forth. The primary goal of these calls is to ensure the best possible outcomes for patients. They also decrease preventable readmissions, which are costly for hospitals.

Anyway, every department in the hospital wanted to start making these calls at the same time. The decision was made to start with one nursing unit at a time. Better to have one area at a time start making the calls. That way leaders could see where the problems were, harvest best practices to use later when subsequent departments started making the calls, and so forth. Starting small is always better than trying to bite off way too much at one time. When this happens, organizations suffer big failures, and people lose faith in their ability to make any change. This is a similar process to taking it one block at a time when revitalizing communities and neighborhoods.

I hear from CEOs of companies that are trying to grow but are struggling. It is often because their scope is too broad. They have too many products. Once they get narrower in scope, it's easier to get back on track.

When a community moves forward with small, methodical steps, those steps add up to what Malcolm Gladwell calls the tipping point—that point where a series of small changes becomes big enough to cause a larger, more meaningful change. If we try to do too much too fast, it just doesn't work.

Communities have so many challenges—whether its poverty, hunger, low graduation rates, teenage pregnancy, crime, vacant buildings and deteriorating downtowns, and so on—that it's easy to want to fix all of these things. Yet, if we try to fix everything, we end up fixing nothing.

As we move to get started, we have to realize that this must happen in small, incremental steps. Yes, there will be some big projects, but even these have to be done one step at a time.

Celebrate small wins and create critical mass.

One method for creating critical mass is to generate some small wins to build up people's confidence and enthusiasm. If they see that previous efforts worked and they're excited about the results, they want more of the same. This leads to more wins, which leads to more wins, and suddenly the group reaches the tipping point.

A good way to do this is to focus on building and revitalizing projects in small "circles" that are not too far apart geographically. Here's how it works: Start with one small geographic area and really develop it. Resist the temptation to do anything outside that circle. Once that circle begins to be revitalized, start working on another circle nearby. Then start developing a third circle.

This approach allows projects to be spaced out and generate small wins. This creates buzz and builds up momentum. As more and more businesses move into these areas, they start to get infill between them. The circles will connect and grow together. This happens naturally and organically. Before you know it, what once may have been a dying street has become a busy, vibrant one. This draws more investors.

In the development of downtown Pensacola, Deborah Dunlap was our trailblazer. She renovated an old building downtown and put residential space in the top and retail shops in the bottom. She started us off!

Early on, at the south end of Palafox Street, the Bodacious Olive store opened and Jewelers Trade Shop was renovated to look like something you'd see in Manhattan. Elebash's Jewelers followed suit. These were small wins, but they really inspired others. People would walk in to these places and say, "Wow! I can't believe this is in Pensacola!" The idea is to create nice places that tell a neighborhood or community, "You are worth it." People want to be proud of their community.

There was an old vacant Masonic temple that a couple of young investors (Harry and Evan Levin) bought and turned it into a music venue called Vinyl Music Hall. (It was similar to The Orange Peel in Asheville.) This brought live music downtown on a regular basis, which was vital. Joe Abston came in and started Hopjacks, which is a bar and pizza place, and a restaurant called The Tin Cow to go with New York Nick's (now NYN's Badlands Roadside Bar), which had been there forever. With just a few new businesses and restaurants, the entertainment district grew.

None of these were huge conglomerates, but all small wins that created a lot of buzz. The north end of Palafox and Garden Streets became more of a bar and entertainment scene, with some retail mixed in. The south end of Palafox and Main Streets became a restaurant and retail location, which worked nicely with Don Alans and Scout and a restaurant called Jackson's. (Luckily, some local businesses had not left, and things began to fill in around them.) In the middle, we ended up getting World of Beer and Old Hickory Whiskey Bar, and more retail spots moved in to join Meadows' Jewelers.

All of this activity created infill, and eventually the north end and south end started to touch.

Palafox had gotten pretty busy, and it seemed to happen quickly. It's not easy to get a place on Palafox anymore, and it was recently named one of the "Ten Great Streets in America" by the American Planning Association. Not bad for a place that was dying just a decade earlier.

This is a great example of how a lot of small wins add up to big ones. Notice how our circles started to touch and create infill. As areas start getting built up, you begin to see there's a critical mass.

Be realistic. This takes time.

In Pensacola the revitalization process gained momentum in 2004. Each year, success builds on success.

Celebrate early wins. Get momentum going and keep it going. There are no quick fixes here.

In Janesville, WI—whose economy was devastated by the loss of its General Motors plant in 2009—the effects are paying off. It is slowly revitalizing.

They removed a big parking plaza that overlooked part of the river, opening up river access. Now they're building a town square on the riverfront. But how long did this take? It took years. It took a lot of push. It took a lot of partnership. And between now and then, Janesville had some small wins along the path leading to this new town square. In the past few months, they have raised $3 million for ARISE, which is what they call their downtown efforts.

Next, we'll talk about what happens after the small wins get things moving. The momentum has been started; the key is to keep it going. And that probably means changing the thinking patterns that the community has settled into over time. It's not always easy to convince people that they can do better and that they deserve better—but that is the true job of every leader.

CHAPTER 7

Getting Momentum and Keeping It Going

In the previous chapter, we talked about small wins and critical mass. Early victories are essential for getting change moving. People get excited when they see progress. But to really build momentum and keep it going, small wins aren't enough. It's also important to break the old thinking patterns that keep a community from expecting and pursuing excellence.

Job one is changing the way people see themselves. Ken Ford—founder and CEO of the Florida Institute for Human & Machine Cognition and one of the early drivers of Pensacola's revitalization—once said Pensacola had so much potential, perhaps more than they even fully realized.

As a change leader, it's important to reiterate that it doesn't matter how things were done in the past. While sharing the good, it's important to also point out that things *can* be better in the future. Identify the things that need to get better and explain why. If not, this attitude of "we are okay where we are" will be a stumbling block that keeps change from happening.

Another common momentum blocker is waiting for perfection. People feel that all the stars have to be perfectly aligned before plans can be implemented. Don't let perfect be the enemy of good. Let people see that there is a commitment to making real progress this time. If we wait until everything is perfect to move forward, nothing will ever get done. We'll never get to 100 percent, and that's okay. Eighty percent is enough.

Years ago, when I was speaking at a large healthcare organization, they brought in a nationally known consulting group called McKinsey & Company. I was able to listen to their speaker before my talk. One of the things the McKinsey speaker said to guard against is getting so caught up in perfection that we don't get into traffic. Think about how chaotic and uneven traffic patterns can be. If we wait for the perfect time and the perfect situation to pull out into the street, we'll never get anywhere. Once in the traffic, adjustments can be made. It's like moving into a new home. No matter how well planned it is, there are always adjustments once we move in.

Just remember: Creating momentum is about taking action, but it's also about communicating about that action. How we communicate is just as important as what we do.

Communicating About the Project

When starting to take action, it's important to bring the community into the loop at every juncture. Educating the community helps get them engaged. Full engagement is a must, and it's difficult to achieve this unless details are communicated the right way. There's never going to be a time when everyone thinks it's communicated perfectly, but do your best.

A big part of driving momentum is creating positive energy. It really helps to be positive and upbeat, even when there is failure (in fact, especially when something goes wrong).

There are going to be some projects that just don't work. For example, with the Community Maritime Park, the original plan was to have a maritime museum. As we talked about it later, it was decided it would be difficult to sustain under the circumstances and the university decided not to move forward with the project. This is a great example of a project with good intentions from all parties that just didn't happen. This was a major change to the overall plan. We did not let that stop our progress or dampen our enthusiasm for the rest of the project. These setbacks can't be allowed to shut down progress. Sadly, there will be people who jump on these setbacks, concentrate on the negative, and focus on that one thing that didn't work. The good news is there's still a park, and there are a lot of wins, but some will focus so hard on what's wrong that they totally miss what's right. As a community, it's important to bring the focus back to the positive.

In trying to get the University of West Florida downtown (a second time), the goal was to build a daycare center, additional office space on one parcel of the Community Maritime Park, and a conference center on another parcel. The keystone of the project was a facility that would house classes from the University of West Florida. The idea was to create a Center for Entrepreneurship. This would bring lots of people to that area, particularly young people, and serve as a great catalyst for change on the west side of Pensacola.

The guidelines that had been laid out were carefully followed, there was $20 million worth of private investment, and it was going to be a great source of property taxes. It appeared to be a win-win. Unfortunately, as things unfolded, the city leadership at the time disagreed and wanted to change the leasing template, so the deal fell apart. This was a significant setback for our community, but we didn't give up. We didn't take it personally, but instead stayed focused on our original goal and started looking for other ways to bring the University of West Florida downtown.

When it appears to be a great project and lots of terrific planning and hard work have been involved, these disappointments can be unsettling, mostly because they're so surprising. Emotions will likely run high for a while. Not everybody's going to agree on how to move forward. Certainly there were people on both sides who were upset about the University of West Florida and the maritime museum. Certainly the people with the Center for Entrepreneurship had a different impression of the city leaders. The reality is these disagreements just have to play out. Sometimes they're going to get a little uglier in the media than anyone wants, but they're going to happen.

However, at the end of the day, it's vital to come back together. If either side says, "I'm going to take my ball and go home," the progress in the community will suffer. Both sides have to be willing to stay on the field and keep a civil working relationship. By always conducting yourself with a lot of civility throughout the process, it makes it easier for everyone to come back together and work as a community toward common goals.

In his book, *The Four Agreements*, don Miguel Ruiz gives four good rules for dealing with these situations:

1. Be impeccable with your word.

2. Don't take anything personally.

3. Don't make assumptions.

4. Always do your best.[1]

These rules help keep us civil and keep relationships in a place where everyone can come back together in the end. Remember, at the end of the day, even those on opposing sides of a referendum are still neighbors trying to do what's best for the community. If things get nasty and resentment sets in, it's not likely that a team can stay focused on their objectives. It's easy to start doing things for the wrong reasons. This negativity not only saps focus away from the goal, but is also sure to bring down the momentum built up by those critical early wins.

Another component is transparency. We talked about this earlier in the book, but it bears repeating here. Transparency creates trust, which generates momentum and keeps it going. Sadly, transparency is getting a bad name. While people and organizations say they are transparent, often they are not. Claiming to be transparent isn't enough. The only way to really build trust is to be honest about motivations and be willing to explain the whole story. Being willing to show the financials of a deal also goes a long way. Sometimes this worries people, as there is this perception that if anyone makes money, it's not good. In community investments, people often assume there is much more money being made than there actually is. In fact, depending on how the stock market is doing, many times the investor would get a better ROI in the stock market instead of the community.

When trying to create a vibrant community, the key message points have to stay front and center. In Pensacola, every time we spoke, we tried to say, "Here's what we want to do. We want to keep those businesses that get outside revenue, we want to invest in those that can grow, and we want to create a vibrant downtown. We want to do all of these things so we can be a community where our children and grandchildren will be able to work and will want to live."

It's easy to get sidetracked and get in the weeds, but it won't happen when people get focused around a few specific goals. Constantly reminding people of what the goals are and explaining the reasoning behind them helps to keep everyone focused.

For example, when we were talking to various groups about the Maritime Park, we always connected the dots. "We want to keep talent here in Pensacola. People told us they want access to water. If we can build this park, we will give them access to water. Also, this park will attract investment, which will create a more vibrant downtown. It will bring a lot of people downtown, and we'll get retail and entertainment. Then we'll get office buildings. And then we'll get places to live. A more vibrant downtown will create more opportunities for people to stay here, and it will attract people who have already left back to the community."

Hitting the main message points over and over and over again keeps them at the front of everyone's mind. They cannot be said too many times.

Remember, though, that communication is a two-way street. When change advocates speak, they *will* get feedback, and it won't always be positive. It's very important to be a good listener and to keep an open mind about what people have to say. Just be prepared for some critical feedback.

Don't let critical feedback stifle momentum.

Few people enjoy hearing critical feedback, and it's especially tough when a lot of what is being said is unfair or untrue. In fact, people are going to be misinformed and say things that are simply not true. To help combat this, we actually put together a document during the Maritime Park campaign detailing myths and facts.

Try not to react to everything. As Vice Admiral Jack Fetterman always said, "Keep your powder dry." This means don't squander resources on attacks that don't matter. It's better to save them for when they are really needed.

Social media makes it easier for people to attack. There are going to be blogs and Facebook posts that are upsetting and drive everyone on the team crazy, because they're not going to be true. Local media may also get involved. I used to have people come up and say, "Did you listen to the radio?" (One particular announcer took aim at me on a daily basis.) And I would say, "No. Why would I listen to him blast me every day?"

We're all human and we all get upset when people criticize or slander us. But it's important to be aware of when reactions are emotional, and not let them derail things. It's easy to quit when people are negative, but that's the last thing a team trying to drive change should do.

Instead, do an honest evaluation of circumstances. This is where a good team comes in handy. Having a solid team around can help regain perspective and separate "emotion" from "reality." As a team, you'll be able to stop and ask, "Hey, are we still doing the right thing? Do we need to change our course?" It's also important to own up to mistakes.

Eventually the community will start having some success, and this will generate its own momentum. Why? Because people will become more trusting and more willing to get behind the effort.

Success builds trust.

After the first success, every other project will get much easier. Once people know how the process works, they start to have confidence. It reminds me of the Green Bay Packers. My wife is a huge Green Bay Packers fan, and, of course, she was in love with Brett Favre. (In fact, she and her girlfriend once drove to Kiln, MS, just to see the community where he was raised.)

When the Green Bay Packers leadership announced that it was going to start Aaron Rodgers ahead of Brett Favre, the Green Bay nation went wild. This was just terrible. This was bad. Well, after the Packers won the Super Bowl with Aaron Rodgers, people weren't questioning leadership's decision nearly as much. Sometimes criticism will not subside until success becomes apparent.

The first big push is the hardest one, because that's the one where the team truly faces the unknown. It's the unknown that creates the fear. And as Neale Donald Walsch said, FEAR is just an acronym for False Evidence Appearing Real. Particularly in the early stages, it's important not to let false evidence derail progress.

A good way to safeguard against this is to keep communicating why things are being done and what the goal is, always connecting the dots so people understand what you are trying to do. It's better to err on the side of over-communicating. Remember, the key message points can never be said too many times.

Keep results in front of people.

Results speak for themselves, as long as they are meaningful. Communicating results effectively means more than just generating reports. As we talked about in the Creating a Tailored Approach for Your City chapter, creating easy-to-read dashboards with measurable results goes a long way. In Pensacola we regularly ran our results in the newspaper and posted them on the Studer Community Institute website.

Confusing activity with outcomes or progress is a common mistake when reporting results. It's often easy to have a flurry of activity, but there also has to be a good, objective way to measure progress and make sure everything stays on track. An effective team always has to be willing to stop doing what doesn't work. Sometimes that's hard because it might mean admitting that a strategy isn't working out as planned. It's okay to be wrong, but it's better to admit it and change course as quickly as possible. Also, there will be times when things are stuck and can't seem to get moving again. At these times, it helps a lot to know what is negotiable and what isn't. If possible, reaching a compromise will help keep things moving. A strong connection to measurable outcomes will help keep things on track.

Throughout all of this, it's important that citizens feel good about their community. It is this good feeling—that the hard work is paying off—that keeps momentum going.

Focus on and promote community pride early in the game.

Vibrant communities are communities that care about themselves. This is why it's important to foster a sense of pride up front. It energizes people, strengthens their sense of identity with the community, and makes them feel they have a vested interest in working together to meet common goals. Being able to jumpstart that sense of identity and pride early on is so important, as that is half the battle.

One big way to do this is by managing up the community and teaching others to do the same. What is being said? Are they welcoming and engaging to each other and to visitors? We have scouts for major league baseball who regularly visit Pensacola to watch Wahoo games. They talk about how much they love the city and how well they are treated not only at the ball park but at restaurants and other places as well. They've become ambassadors for the city. We go out of our way to make that happen. Each scout receives a welcome letter from me, with my cellphone number if they need anything. We do a survey while they're there to make sure everything's going well, and they get a $25 gift certificate to spend downtown.

Another way to promote community pride is to talk often and enthusiastically about your community's story. Every great city has an interesting story to tell. It's important to identify this early on, define it, share it, and teach it to other stakeholders. It's up to the citizens to tell the story of their community.

Pensacola has a very rich history and a great story to tell. In Pensacola, some bar and restaurant owners have worked this into their business identity. Great taxi drivers will tell you interesting stories as you ride through town. Once people know to do this and know that others are interested in learning about their community, they truly enjoy sharing their story.

In general, are citizens positive? Do they say good things about their community? Or do they tear it down? Making sure residents know the importance of managing up their city really helps to build a positive brand. This is especially important for people who have face-to-face contact with visitors: taxi drivers, restaurant workers, etc. These are people visitors look to for suggestions. It's worthwhile to help these folks learn how to showcase what people might want to see.

Leadership should really take the lead on creating this positive attitude. This means communicating positive stories as often as possible. A good strategy is to work with the media to share the town's success stories: projects that are happening, awards that are being won, and so forth. People really respond to positivity. They want to hear good news. And when they hear it, they will share it with others. Remember, positivity is contagious!

Finally, never declare victory.

The work of creating a vibrant community is never done. That's why it's critical never to declare victory, but to use success to create more enthusiasm and grow the project base. Once the community starts having success, everyone starts feeling good about the community, and it becomes easy to keep the less successful projects from bringing down momentum by focusing on the future. The message is, "We've proven we can do great things. We did this and this, so we can also meet this other goal."

We've talked a lot about gaining momentum and keeping it going. No doubt much of the early wins and the positive energy that's generated from them will center on the downtown area. A vibrant downtown is the epicenter of a vibrant community. In the next chapter we will discuss why downtowns are so important—and how to do everything possible to make it a place where people want to work, live, and play.

CHAPTER 8

Start With Downtown

In revitalizing a community, what's the best way to determine where to start geographically? In most cases it makes sense to rebuild downtown first and let everything expand from there. After all, a great downtown is a requirement now for attracting young talent. People judge an entire city or community by its downtown. It's the heart and soul and the image to show the world.

When a community starts building a vibrant downtown, it gets people activated and sparks growth in the rest of the community. As citizens start seeing great buildings and new businesses, their enthusiasm builds. They want to see more growth. And they want to be part of it. It's also great for the tax base. High-density projects create more investments per square foot than other projects.

Other businesses will start to grow and prosper around it. For instance, in Pensacola there was a small co-op grocery store downtown named Ever'man Co-operative. As downtown grew, so did it.

Historically, downtowns were widely recognized as the heart of a community. But sometime around the 1950s and '60s many of America's downtowns began a long period of decline. Public policy, market forces, and the growth of the suburbs—fueled by post-World War II economic expansion; America's love affair with the automobile; and a desire for cleanliness, space, and safety—caused people to leave the city in droves. Over time, many downtowns were abandoned and boarded up.

But now the pendulum is swinging back. People realize again how important a great downtown really is.

The reasons for the comeback of the downtown are complex, but in general, our society's tastes and preferences are changing. More and more people are drawn to the livability and walkability of a vibrant downtown. Many no longer want the hassle of car ownership (and cars are no longer a status symbol).

It's also noteworthy that sharp divisions between work and personal time no longer exist. Thanks in large part to technology, many of us can work anytime, from anywhere. It makes sense that people would want to live, work, play, and socialize all in the same place. Downtowns, with their color, energy, diversity, and cultural amenities, are the perfect solution.

There are many reasons a community should make creating a vibrant downtown a priority. Here are just a few of them:

- A vibrant downtown is a living symbol of a community's economic health, history, and local quality of life.

- Great downtowns attract talent and business growth. They retain and create jobs, which leads to a stronger tax base. (Great downtowns protect the property values not only of commercial buildings but of surrounding residential areas as well.)

- They nurture new small businesses, which are the building blocks of a healthy economy. Entrepreneurs often can't afford malls and strip malls, but they might be able to afford a downtown location.

- They reduce sprawl. Building up instead of out is a wiser use of community resources like infrastructure and tax dollars.

- They have beautiful old historic buildings that are often more desirable to business owners, residents, and visitors than new construction.

- They appeal to young people, in particular, who want a walkable city with lots of great restaurants, shops, exciting activities, and cool residential areas.

Think of a vibrant downtown as a three-legged stool, with the legs being live, work, and play. All three of these activities combine to create a sense of place.

There are four main ingredients that must come together to create a vibrant downtown: programming, retail/entertainment, office space, and residential. We'll discuss each of them in more detail below.

Ingredient 1: Programming

Programming should be the first priority, as it is what actually draws people to the area. The goal is to get citizens and visitors alike to hang out downtown so they'll shop, eat, drink, and possibly even stay overnight. But they need a reason to come downtown. The community has to create events that draw them there.

For example, in Pensacola we have a multi-use stadium, home of the Pensacola Blue Wahoos. The park is a great venue for music and other special events. We also have the annual Seafood Festival, which attracts more than 10,000 people to our downtown area over three days.

The Downtown Improvement Board, a local merchants association, started a Saturday farmers market on Palafox Street that always attracts huge crowds. They also sponsor all kinds of events downtown. For example, one Friday night a month, the streets are closed downtown for Gallery Night, which features music, art, and cuisine. Downtown is also home to many running clubs and fundraising walks.

These are just some examples of the programming that can create a vibrant downtown. For other communities, programming might take the form of a YMCA, a theater, or a series of concerts.

Here are a few tips to consider:

Create a regularly occurring public event that showcases downtown business. This makes people aware of merchants, restaurants, musicians, artists, and other service providers such as massage therapists, fitness centers, photographers, and so forth. The event might be a farmers market or an art walk.

Look for inexpensive ways to drive traffic during the off-season. Holiday activities are always popular. In Pensacola, the Downtown Improvement Board started a First City Lights Festival for the holidays. Once you get the logistics such as parking worked out, you can use the same formula for other events, such as a New Year's Eve street party and trick-or-treating at downtown stores and restaurants.

Consider permanent structures to accommodate outdoor open markets. Not only will this allow events to occur rain or shine, it solidifies their significance in the culture of the community.

Develop public gathering places that make people feel welcome. Parks, plazas, and public squares are people magnets. Outdoor seating is always good; remember, the idea is to make people comfortable so they will hang around awhile. Include well-lighted areas for night walking.

Invite street musicians to play on weekends. Public music adds color and richness to downtown. It lifts people's spirits and may even put them in a shopping mood. And of course, the musicians appreciate the exposure.

Build a downtown playground or interactive water features. Downtowns already attract single and young professionals, so these features are a good way to become more family-friendly.

Focus marketing efforts on activities and the feelings they create. People are more attracted to things to do than places to go.

Consider a downtown bike share program. This hits the trends toward healthier lifestyles and greener living.

Once a community gets intentional about giving people a reason to come downtown, it all starts to blossom. People find they enjoy being there. They discover stores they didn't know about and they try out restaurants. Best of all, they come back.

Ingredient 2: Retail and Entertainment

Programming is just one part of the formula. When people are downtown for a farmers market or a music festival, they need places to eat and shop. A vibrant downtown gives them those places.

Think about why Disney created Disney Springs. People come for the theme parks, but they also want to shop, eat, drink, and otherwise spend money on entertainment. Disney wanted to capture that spending.

Of course, in most cases there won't be a huge corporation financing a shopping/dining/retail district. Communities need to attract owners of restaurants, boutique shops, coffee houses, and so forth and entice them to open up downtown. But it won't necessarily happen on its own. The process needs to be deliberately cultivated.

Remember that downtown is more than just a destination. Residents and visitors need to feel that being downtown is an experience. There has to be a "there." And creating that sense of "there" is an art and a science.

Here are a few tips for doing so:

Be strategic about which types of businesses are placed at street level. Realtors, attorneys, and accountants should not be on the first level. Put them up higher. Street level should be reserved for restaurants, shops, and other retail establishments. This helps generate foot traffic.

Consider zoning the entertainment district. When making decisions about where to place businesses, think carefully about categories. Be balanced and strategic about where you entice people to walk, and that means shops, restaurants, entertainment venues, and other retailers need to be grouped together. Try to avoid creating a mishmash of businesses that don't complement each other: like an attorney's office next to an eyeglass place, next to a bar, next to a consignment shop, next to three art studios.

In Pensacola, young entrepreneur Katie Garrett wanted to put a whiskey bar in an available space. The size was right but it was not the right fit for that particular street, which was filled with family-friendly businesses like a food court, a hair salon, a flower shop, etc. We ended up helping Katie find a better location, across from a craft beer store and right down the street from a theater. She loved this new location and it worked out great for her. (And as it turned out, a nail salon went into the spot she originally wanted. It was a much better fit.)

In fact, in both 2015 and 2016 *The Bourbon Review* listed the Old Hickory Whiskey Bar as one of the Best Bourbon Bars in America. It has also been featured in *Southern Living* and *Southwest: The Magazine*. Katie herself has become a rock star. She speaks regularly at the University of West Florida and other events helping other young entrepreneurs achieve their own dreams.

Here's another example. We have Bodacious Brew, which is a coffee shop, and So Chopped, which is a salad bar, on one side of Palafox Street. Initially, golf pro Bubba Watson wanted to open his candy store on the same side. However, the other side of the street was a better fit because there was a clothing store and a jewelry store over there that were desperate to get foot traffic. Bubba always puts the community first, so he was happy to move his store to the other side of the street. It turned out to be a great decision for him and for downtown.

That's a way to program a downtown. Thinking strategically is key. Where do people walk? Where are they going to go after they eat dinner? Where are they going to sit? It's about deliberately and purposely moving people toward the places you want them to go.

Give part of downtown a name. This makes it feel like a destination, not just a place. For example, Manhattan has SoHo, which of course stands for South of Houston Street. Pensacola created the SOGO district for South of Government Street.

Focus on great gathering places. When downtown Asheville started reinventing itself, they thought about what types of businesses would encourage people to gather and hang around. They sought out bookstores and coffee shops (with WiFi, of course).

Invest in retail beautification. Think of curb appeal. Window boxes with flowers and greenery and attractive signage extend the business onto the sidewalk and invite people in. This goes a long way toward attracting first-time shoppers to restaurants and stores.

Spell out in lease agreements that businesses must be open late. The Destination Development Association says that 70 percent of consumer retail spending takes place after 6:00 p.m.[1] This makes sense, because visitors want something to do at night other than sitting in a hotel room watching TV. (Speaking of which, if shops are open later, hotel occupancy increases by 30 percent, which is a great byproduct.)

Ingredient 3: Office Space

While the retail businesses attract the foot traffic, downtowns also need realtors, accountants, attorneys, architects, and other types of non-retail businesses to help support the economy. Cities need to attract both types.

Non-retail companies keep downtown activated during the day. Employees who work for them, and also their customers, become customers for the retail companies.

Of course, the benefits go both ways. There are plenty of reasons why businesses want to be located in a vibrant downtown. For instance:

Downtown is conveniently located. It's easy for employees and customers to get to, especially if the city has a good transportation system.

It offers a great talent base. Lots of Millennials and young professionals are attracted to downtown. They either already live there or they really want to. Young people have a certain energy and enthusiasm that businesses want.

There's a built-in culture and plenty to do. For example, vibrant downtowns have lots of exciting restaurants nearby to take clients to and lots of entertainment options to help employees stay energized.

They are surrounded by potential customers and tons of networking opportunities. People are more likely to patronize businesses that they see every day. And it's easy to form partnerships with other businesses in close proximity.

The energy of downtown breeds innovation. Any time a lot of people get together and exchange ideas it sets the stage for great innovation. This is exactly what downtown offers, and it's exactly what businesses need.

Ingredient 4: Residential

Residential development is important, because if things get tough economically, there will still be a base of people to support restaurants, shops, and other businesses. Getting residential downtown can be sort of a challenge, though. It would be ideal if residential and office space development came first and then retail. Retail and entertainment would go through the roof. But it doesn't really work that way.

People don't want to move downtown if there is nothing for them to do there. What happens is little bakeries and bridal shops and coffee houses come first. They are the early movers because they're making decisions with their hearts and their passion, certainly not with analytics. For a while, they're barely making it. All it takes is a couple of weekends of bad weather or a shift in the economy, and they're in big trouble.

So how does one bring residential downtown? The challenge is that the most profitable residential is expensive residential, and expensive residential doesn't get the critical mass downtown. There might be nine condos, but that's only nine people living there. There needs to be a variety of residential. Asheville, NC, was fortunate to have these big old buildings that could be turned into apartments, but every town doesn't have that.

What most towns need to do is start with local investors. National or regional investors are going to be concerned with return on investment. In Pensacola, the ROI on our first apartment building was 7.6 percent. We needed local investors because they saw that the real ROI is a better community.

Who benefits from this investment in residential? The real winners are all those early movers—those people who opened retail businesses that they feel passionate about. In essence, this is rewarding them for taking that risk.

When you walk around a city, and residential is coming, you can just feel it. That's a big turning point in the creation of a vibrant downtown. And once the first wave of residential comes, the next wave comes on top of it. And once people start living downtown, businesses are much better prepared to deal with a bad economy.

Right now in Pensacola, we have 258 units downtown as part of Southtowne community. That's 450 people. All these people are living here every day, and they're attracting more businesses. And what happens is people sell their homes and move into infrastructure that already exists. The houses they sold, which may be close to downtown, are also opening up. The beauty of this is that it creates more tax structure with less infrastructure. Then, the new infrastructure comes when there's better community solvency. This is solid, organic growth. In the last five years, the Community Redevelopment Agency (CRA) has gone from an assessed property value of $675 million to $850 million, which equates to 25.9 percent growth. Also, there are 14 projects worth $100 million being built downtown right now not included in this total.

More and more, people want to live where their job is. Changing trends in work/life blend mean that people work all hours. Living downtown means they can be near their office and avoid the long commute. They can grab a quick bite somewhere and go back to work. The fact that many downtowns build condos and loft apartments on the upper story (above businesses and retail establishments) makes this kind of lifestyle easier.

It's important to keep in mind that there are two age groups that want to live downtown: under 35s and over 55s. Young people like downtown living for the reasons we've already discussed, and they don't have kids so they don't need big backyards and lots of space. Empty nesters like downtown because it offers freedom from yard maintenance and upkeep. They can walk everywhere—the grocery store, the bank, the park, the clinic. And being in the middle of the action means they can stay vital and engaged.

Remember these two groups when building out residential and look for ways to meet their needs. Others want to come downtown to visit, but these are the folks who want to live there.

A Few Other Lessons We've Learned from Our Downtown Journey

As we've worked to revitalize downtown Pensacola, we've learned many lessons in what to do, what not to do, and how to approach problems that cropped up. Here are just a few takeaways:

Every city has a story. Figure out what it is and help residents tell it. For example, Pensacola has a lot of history and that's a big part of our story. Figuring out what sets the community apart is a good place to start when planning a vibrant downtown. That should be the centerpiece of the town's vision statement.

Be firm in dealing with code violations. Nothing puts a damper on development like an old dilapidated building in the middle of a vibrant community.

Deal properly with large vacant properties that won't move. Sometimes people sit on unused property as the area around them starts to develop so they can command a higher price when selling. Vacant buildings put a damper on development and shouldn't be allowed.

Get property owners all working together. Many downtowns have property owners who don't work together with a common vision. There might be some absentee owners. To be most effective, they need to all work together with a common vision.

Create one great intersection. In The Pensacola Story chapter, we talked about the importance of having a great intersection downtown. Early on, decide which intersection is best to build out. This takes a lot of thought, and the answer is not always obvious.

Ray Gindroz from Urban Design Associates helped us determine that Palafox and Main was the right intersection for Pensacola. At the time, all I saw were two buildings that had been vacant for 20 or 30 years and two vacant pieces of property. One might think some smart person would've come and done something already, but no, those buildings and empty lots were just sitting there.

Before settling on Palafox and Main, we had also talked about other intersections. One had a big federal building, and Ray explained that this is really not the best situation for an intersection. Another one seemed nice, but it had four lanes of traffic moving too quickly.

He just felt that Palafox and Main was the right place to develop. We were fortunate enough to buy one of the vacant pieces of property, and Rishy ended up putting her olive oil store, chopped salad shop, coffee shop, and kitchen store there.

Change one-way streets to two-way streets. This is another point we learned from Ray Gindroz. In fact, Palafox, which was named one of the "Ten Great Streets in America" by the American Planning Association, used to be one-way. Ray told us that you don't want to speed traffic up; you want to slow it down. A traffic jam isn't the worst thing in the world. People will pull over and they will get used to it. It's much worse for downtown to have no traffic.

Sidewalks are vitally important to life in a community. They encourage walking and act as pipelines for pedestrian movement. They build connectivity, shape the appearance of a community, and make it more enjoyable to socialize out on the street downtown.

Utilize existing structures whenever possible. While it's tempting to build new and shiny, many downtowns have wonderful old buildings that could be revitalized. (We have had a lot of success with this in Pensacola.) Utilize these buildings when possible. Not only does it preserve history and capture the character of a community, but it also helps maximize existing infrastructure, which is a far more efficient use of funds. This is both an art and a science. Some old buildings will work out wonderfully; some will need to go.

Focus on street thickening. Incremental development—focusing on one block at a time—is much more sustainable than urban sprawl. The magic bullet for building cities is small investments over a long period of time. Small, low-risk, high-return projects can really improve neighborhoods and impact people's lives.

Look for underutilized land and fill in. Density is the goal. Look for those holes and fill them in. In Pensacola we focused on building and revitalizing projects in small "circles" that were not too far apart geographically. Here's how it works: Start with one small geographic area and really develop it. Resist the temptation to do anything outside that circle. Once that circle begins to be revitalized, start working on another circle nearby. Then start developing a third circle.

Pockets of activity will start to develop. As more and more businesses move into these areas, others will start to fill in the areas in between. The circles will connect and grow together. This happens naturally and organically. Before you know it, what once may have been a dying street has become a busy, vibrant one.

Get part of a university downtown. This is a great bonus. Universities create constant revenue streams. They continue to do well even when the economy is doing poorly. Also, they often spin off intellectual capital in the community. Often universities are motivated to move downtown. For example, Tampa moved its medical school downtown because that is where young people want to be. Aggressively recruit colleges like you would a company.

Don't let parking issues hold up progress. Sometimes parking issues can be a deterrent to developers. Don't let it be. Parking will always be an issue so move ahead anyway. Honestly, if developers focus on creating a walkable city, people will be okay with walking. Plus, entrepreneurs can help solve parking issues. For example, in Pensacola a lack of parking spurred a boutique cab business.

Public restrooms are important. People visiting downtowns need public restrooms. Without them, people go into restaurants just to use the restroom and don't buy anything. So what if they need to be staffed? The downtown improvement board can do that, as they'll be making a lot more money from having more people shopping downtown.

Tourists love a great downtown. A vibrant downtown can really drive tourism dollars into your local economy. But be careful not to overly focus on tourism, as it is too sensitive to economic swings. The main point to remember is to focus on creating a great place to live for residents. When you do that, tourism follows naturally and organically. Downtowns also attract regional tourism, which can yield a great economic boost. A day of shopping and dining makes for a great little getaway for those who live within driving distance.

Make sure you are showcasing all the things visitors can do. Include restaurants, hotels, retailers, and other businesses, not to mention your community's natural attractions and fun events. Check out www.visitpensacola.com. Run by Steve Hayes, this site makes it easy for visitors to see all the great things Pensacola has to offer. It's worth noting that downtown Pensacola was named the 2017 Great Places of Florida People's Choice Winner, following a poll administered by the American Planning Association of Florida.

It's better to grow up than out. People fear building up. They think in extremes, and when they hear talk about building up instead of out, they assume it means jumping from no high rises to giant high rises everywhere. They also fear density, but this fear is also unfounded.

Ironically, density may have gotten a bad rap from environmentalists who didn't like the look of tall buildings. What has happened over the years is that by avoiding density, many communities have created huge storm water issues by building these giant flat surface parking lots that aren't porous. That has hurt the environment. It's also created urban sprawl, which forces people to drive instead of walk.

The truth is, tall buildings aren't bad. Vertical growth is good for both the environment and for the local tax base. And when you start doing the numbers, the reason why becomes clear. Pensacola's Maritime Place office building is a good example. It's 77,000 square feet on four stories. We had a height restriction of 70 feet, so we were able to build it up four stories.

Now, if the building had been kept at one story, the property tax would have been maybe $60,000 or $80,000 a year. But because they were able to go up four stories, Pensacola is able to collect more than $200,000 in property tax and it takes up pretty much the same amount of green space. Plus it's a beautiful building.

The lesson is that it's important to have good planning and a good sense of balance. No city has to go to extremes. Eventually, communities find they can't afford the sprawl and they have to either go up or out. In general, most of the time they're better off going up.

Downtown is where the lion's share of the focus, development, and renovation need to happen. Investing here pays off in a big way. A great downtown gives citizens from all walks of life and all parts of the community a place to connect.

It's truly a point of pride that everyone can share. And in many ways, a vibrant downtown becomes the engine that powers the rest of the project. Once things really start popping downtown, momentum spreads to other areas, and the city will be well on its way to becoming a community where people love to live, work, and play.

CHAPTER 9

Little Things Make a Big Difference

Why don't communities make the necessary changes? Often, it's for the same reasons individuals don't. When many changes are needed, getting started feels overwhelming. It's hard to know where to begin. Even if a community does know, they may not have a big budget to fund everything they need, so they just stay stuck.

The good news is that meaningful change doesn't have to be huge and expensive. If you've ever owned a home, you know that a fresh coat of paint can really improve how things look and feel. There are relatively affordable and easy solutions that can make a huge difference.

Communities can also take the "coat of paint" approach to change. Simple, quick fixes can make a big impact. And sometimes this is all that's needed to generate some excitement, get the change mindset going, and build the momentum we talked about earlier in the book.

Charles "Chuck" Marohn is the founder and president of Strong Towns, which is a media organization leading a national movement to rethink how American cities are built to help them become strong, resilient, and prosperous. Chuck was the first speaker we brought in for Pensacola's CivicCon series. He talked about how tempting it is for communities to build "new stuff," but emphasized that it's better to fix what's broken first.

Chuck made a comparison to a homeowner receiving a big windfall of cash. The roof on his house is falling in and desperately needs repairs. But the homeowner decides to use his funds to build on an addition before mending the roof.

Communities do this, too. When thinking about making improvements, their first impulse might be to start with a new project. But it makes more financial and psychological sense to fix what is broken first.

A few tips for getting started:

Slow down and really look at what most needs fixing. Chuck suggested taking a slow drive through your neighborhood. When you take the time to experience your community at 2 mph, not 45 mph, you will see things you've never seen or noticed before.

Once a community knows what needs fixing, they'll often find there are simple things to do that pack a big punch. Just look for ways to make lives better and see where it leads.

Don't choose these fixes at random. Get intentional about the little things that can make a big difference in the community. Observe where people are struggling in their daily lives. Updates like designated street crossings and sidewalks where there were none before can make a big difference. Schools are another great place to start, as they are magnets for life. Go there and observe how people are using the space and ask what can be done to make it better.

A cornerstone of Marohn's philosophy is that it's better to make small, incremental investments over time instead of taking a "big project" approach (which is risky and expensive and can be politically controversial).

In Marohn's hometown of Brainerd, MN, they have a program called "A Better Brainerd" where they are looking to make small incremental changes over time. This non-profit organization looks for small ways that can make people's lives better. These low-cost, high-return investments occur from the bottom up rather than the top down, and they create enduring prosperity for communities.

Here are just a few examples of improvements Strong Towns proposed for Brainerd in 2014, as reported in *Neighborhoods First: A low risk, high return strategy for a better Brainerd*.[1]

- Create bike lanes and reestablish pavement markings with a more neighborhood-friendly design on a street that was previously too wide and dangerous. (Wide streets encourage dangerous speeds.) (Project cost: $5,875)

- Create a pedestrian crosswalk on a busy street people use to get to the only grocery store within walking distance of their neighborhood. To protect foot traffic, paint crosshatch striping throughout the intersection. (Project cost: $850)

- Plant trees in Mill Park. This is the only city park that doesn't require crossing a street (thus, it's the only park that children may safely walk to). Due to its lack of shade, this park is too hot in the summertime. Planting trees would solve that problem, and would also hide an unsightly backdrop to the park. This is a modest investment that will eventually raise property values throughout the neighborhood. (Project cost: $900)

Don't wait until things are broken to get involved. Take notice of what is about to fail or break. Getting out in front of these problems will save money in the long run.

All of these little fixes can have a big impact on community pride and create a sense of ownership and responsibility. But repairs are only the beginning. Being proactive helps build community pride. Here's how:

Look for small, easy ways to make a good first impression on visitors. A big part of building community pride has to do with paying careful attention to how things look. That's why many communities have a "gateway" or at least an attractive sign that creates a sense of place and reflects the ambience of the town.

What is the first thing visitors see when they arrive in the community? Is there a prominent landmark, a beautiful building, or a big piece of public art that creates the feeling that they've arrived at a special destination? If not, maybe there should be. What people see is a big part of creating your brand.

Make sure prominent landmarks look fresh and appealing. If landmarks in the community don't look welcoming and well maintained, then do something about them right away. The way a city is kept says a lot about how its residents see it.

When retired Navy Vice Admiral Jack Fetterman came to Pensacola, he noticed the landmark water tower had peeling paint and suggested they paint it right away. While it's no longer functional, the tower is an iconic symbol of Pensacola, and it's the first thing people see when they come downtown. It serves as a billboard of sorts and appears in so many tourist photos. It deserved to be refurbished and repainted. This was a relatively simple fix that has made a big marketing impact.

Keep the community clean and green. Just keeping a city clean and attractive—and maybe even planting a few flowers—can make a huge difference. There is even a fair amount of evidence that creating a cleaner, greener, better-maintained community can lower crime rates. Certainly, attractive communities have higher property values, attract more businesses, and promote loyalty in citizens.

The great news is that small, carefully thought-out changes can make a big difference in how communities look. People notice these things right away. They spark a big surge of pride. Citizens get excited about their community again, perhaps for the first time in a very long time. And suddenly, they are motivated to make more changes.

Before the citizens even realize it, the city is on its way to becoming a vibrant community—and the goodwill and positive energy of the citizens becomes an incredible source of momentum.

CHAPTER 10

The Role of Government

Government has a valuable role to play in creating vibrant communities. However, the role is moderated by legislative, policy, and budgetary limitations. Recognizing these limitations helps formulate realistic expectations.

Here's what Jim Clifton has to say on this subject in *The Coming Jobs War:*

"In defense of Washington, it wasn't originally set up to be the nation's economic engine. The U.S. government has seeded whole industries through land grant universities, defense contractors, and scientific and medical researchers to name just a few. But the government has never, will never, nor should it be expected to ignite badly needed sustainable economic booms. These economic booms originate in the souls of individuals and great cities. Washington exists for law and order, war and peace, infrastructure, social services, and a wide variety of national and international policies that help hold the country together. But don't look there for sustainable, quality economic growth."[1]

Clifton is writing about the federal government here, but the same is true for local governments. They simply don't have the capacity to revitalize towns, cities, and communities, and that was never intended to be their role. It's difficult for officials to drive things long term. Because they rotate in and out with four-year election cycles, it is difficult to depend on them to maintain continuity. Often big-vision projects take more than one or two election cycles to complete. They require long-term dedication and tenacity in order to execute these projects so they closely resemble the original vision.

It's the same in the business world. Senior executives come and go even as daily client demands, big projects, and initiatives continue. Just as the middle managers are the ones who really set the culture of a company, the residents and small business owners in a community are the middle managers who define and manage the community culture for the long haul.

Money is a big issue as well. In many instances, elected officials do not have access to a budget surplus that can provide needed seed money or investment capital.

In other words, it's time to change the conversation about how we think about the role of government.

In 1996, Dr. Frank Benest, former city manager of Palo Alto, CA, wrote an article in ICMA's *Public Management* magazine in which he used a great metaphor to describe the changing role of government in the community. He said we should move from a vending-machine to a barn-raising mentality. "The barn-raising approach promotes citizen responsibility as opposed to the passive consumption of services. When confronted with a problem, people do not ask, "What is government going to do for us?" Rather, they focus on *"What are we going to do?"*[2]

This is a great way to think of our relationship with local government. We don't put in our tax dollars and wait for goods and services to come to us. Instead, we are partners and active participants. We have to roll up our sleeves and make things happen.

Chuck Marohn, founder and president of Strong Towns, told a wonderful story about a blighted neighborhood in Memphis that took matters into their own hands, after feeling like government was not responsive to their grassroots ideas for revitalization. They painted crosswalks and parking spaces, cleaned up old buildings, and put together a weekend street fair that invited vendors to become permanent tenants. It worked! These citizens revitalized this deserted street with no public dollars and no real government participation. In this unique instance, they proved the endorsement and oversight of government simply were not needed.

So all of that being said, we certainly need government to partner with communities in revitalization efforts. If you're an elected official, what should people expect from you? To follow are just a few guidelines on what local government can and should do.

First and foremost, keep the community clean and safe.

It's just common sense that low crime rates, clean streets, and public spaces are more inviting for citizens, visitors, and entrepreneurs. Business growth accompanies clean, well-illuminated streets. Streetscapes characterized by litter, weed growth, and darkness after sunset will ensure a continuous cycle of blight and short-lived businesses.

Set consistent guidelines regarding public property.

Make sure clear guidelines are developed early on, before you need them. For example, what metrics will be used to make decisions like school districting or use of public property for citizens' use and enjoyment? Government must clearly define the ways public property can be used, the cost of using it, and what's going to happen to it in the future. Keep these guidelines consistent and make sure they are published for easy and constant access. This will earn the faith of business leaders and private citizens, which will in turn attract more entrepreneurs to make investments. Conversely, one of the best ways to lose the faith of private investors in the community is for government officials to keep changing the rules.

Years ago, I was working with a school district, and it became very obvious, due to population shifts, that they were going to have to close a school in the future. It is difficult to adequately imagine how hard this kind of change is for students who attend that school and the students' parents. It creates a lot of anxiety. So the recommendation to the school board was to get people to agree on some concise guidelines regarding how decisions would be made and communicated. This would ensure that when a school closing is imminent, there would be a process to follow, and everyone would know what to expect.

Does that mean people won't be upset? No. They will still be upset. However, they would be much more upset if no guidelines were established and communicated, or if those guidelines were not consistently followed. When expectations are known, you can prepare. And preparation always lessens anxiety, and transparency fosters trust in the process.

Be true to your RFP processes.

Establish the criteria for selecting and evaluating requests for proposals (RFPs) in advance. Make sure everybody knows what they are—from budget considerations to metrics the proposals will be judged on to deadlines for submitting them. Don't change these processes in mid-stream.

Often, communities will issue a request for proposal, and once the bid comes in, they won't follow the guidelines. I was once involved in a bid and was waiting on the final answer when I learned that the process had been extended. If you're going to extend the process, make sure everybody knows it's happening and why. If not, this can look like favoritism—like you changed the rules because somebody said they needed more time.

Create smart zoning rules and clearly define them.

Often private developers and private landowners don't want restrictions on how they can use their property. From their perspective, this is understandable. No one wants to be hindered from selling property if a great offer comes through. The problem with that is, what if it ends up being used for something that hurts the nearby neighbors or the community as a whole?

Zoning is the foundation for strategic growth. A community has to be able to invite flexibility yet foster compatibility. The singular use designation of an area or district is archaic and is not how progressive cities or developments are doing their land planning. However, compatible businesses and occupancies should be grouped together. For example, if a loud bar was placed next door to a children's clothing store, it wouldn't work well for either party.

Make these rules up front and be very clear about them. Will some private owners be a little upset? Yes. But overall, the common good of the community must come first.

Don't make your zoning rules vague. In their book *Switch: How to Change Things When Change Is Hard,* the Heath brothers wrote that most failures stem from ambiguity. You must take all ambiguity out of your zoning, just as you should with your guidelines, your processes, etc.

Be easy to work with.

It's essential for government officials to be available to answer questions and provide guidance to people who want to start a business. This is something Pensacola does very well. Key department leaders make themselves available at a certain time once per week. Business owners and developers can meet with them in a sort of "one-stop shop."

This accessibility goes a long way toward making the process easier. There are a lot of details involved in planning and developing, and decisions need to be made quickly and efficiently (and in the right sequence). Costs normally go up, not down, and you don't want to lose your window of opportunity. Having everyone together at a set time can make a huge difference.

Make sure codes are clearly spelled out and that they make sense. Then enforce them consistently and fairly.

Ambiguous and unenforced codes also deter growth. So it's very important to have them firmly in place. But also, from time to time, we need to ask, *Do our codes make sense and achieve what we want them to achieve for our community?* If the answer is no, then change them.

Once the codes are in place, enforce them. One of the biggest complaints communities have is that there are too many vacant buildings downtown. There are always several businesses that have been written up for years for code violations, but the owners just hang on to them, waiting for the market to flourish so they can get top dollar. No one has made the consequences painful enough to force the owners to act, so these vacant buildings become eyesores.

Finally, know when it makes sense to be flexible.

There are occasions when exceptions are needed and appropriate. Yes, make sure good, solid code enforcement is practiced, but also allow some flexibility as times change and needs evolve.

Don't create a city of exceptions, but don't create a city that's too rigid to utilize reasonable exceptions. Innovation and problem-solving require adaptability. As long as there is transparency and everyone is open about why exceptions are made, most people will understand and respect your decisions.

Ultimately, government officials and private citizens all have a stake in creating a vibrant community. Our roles are very different, but we all want the same outcomes. We all want great neighborhoods to live in, great schools to send our children to, and a thriving economy that provides good jobs for our friends and neighbors.

We need to always remember that whether we work in a government office, own a local business, or work for a local corporation, we are all partners. It takes patience, persistence, and a lot of trust to build these relationships and keep them strong, but when we do, everyone wins.

CHAPTER 11

Focus on Education

A strong education system is a critical part of building a strong community. In fact, it's the foundation for almost everything that will happen in the future.

When we do a good job of teaching the children in our community, we are training tomorrow's workforce. A well-educated workforce is good for local businesses. Many studies show that well-educated workers are more likely to be productive, high performing, law abiding, and healthy. All of this leads to more competitive local companies and a stronger local economy.

For the same reasons, well-educated communities attract investment. Businesses looking to set up shop or relocate favor communities with high graduation rates.

Strong school systems also attract talent. People who are thinking of moving to a community or starting a business in an area will look closely at the quality of the local schools.

Finally, a solid education creates upward social mobility. Children who want to go to college will be well prepared to succeed. Often, they'll end up coming back home to work and may end up settling down and raising their families. And a whole community of well-educated, thriving citizens attracts development and good jobs, which in turn attracts more well-educated, thriving citizens. It's a virtuous cycle.

So how should a community go about starting this cycle? The first item is to evaluate the local education system. This means having a good handle on the metrics as they relate to education. What is the kindergarten readiness score? What is the community's graduation rate? How does the school system rank against others in the state? In the nation? Having the numbers to refer to allows dialogue about the state of education in concrete terms.

As stated earlier in the book, but as a reminder, it's important to keep these metrics on the community's dashboard and in front of the public. Refer to them early and often. This is a good way to keep the focus on the importance of education.

To follow are a few insights and suggestions for improving a community's education system and keeping it strong.

Understand that it takes a village to educate a child.

Every member of the community must be engaged in helping students succeed and grow up to become capable, self-sufficient citizens. This means engaging people who don't currently have school-aged children, business owners, and all others who might otherwise not be involved. If students aren't doing well, *everyone* loses.

Research shows when families, teachers, and the community come together to support student learning, students earn better grades, show up for class more regularly, stay in school longer, and are more likely to enroll in higher-level programs.

So, what are some ways to get the community engaged in improving the local school system? Here are some things we have found to be successful:

Elect a great school board. Great schools begin with great school board members. These people serve as the link between the public schools and the rest of the community. (They're often described as the education "watchdog" for the community.) Find and nurture board members who love working together as a team, strike the right balance between standing up for their own views and listening to others, and don't mind asking the tough questions.

Hire a great superintendent who is a strong leader and hold them accountable for their performance. Use a good evaluation tool to make sure they know what's expected and they understand the priorities. In working with school systems, I've found the best evaluations are transparent and based on objective and weighted "hard" measures: for example, student achievement, employee engagement scores, parent satisfaction, and financial effectiveness.

Encourage volunteering. Volunteerism is the simplest way to get members of the community engaged in our schools and in the lives of our children. Business and local community leaders, charities, civic organizations, and parents can all find a way to give of their time or resources. Here are a few ways people can volunteer:

- Help out in the classroom

- Chaperone a field trip

- Mentor or tutor a child

- Visit and speak to a classroom of children (so they can see a successful businessperson firsthand)

- Donate equipment, school supplies, meals, or sponsor a team at the school

- Fund a program

These are just a few of the ways a community can work together to ensure that children are receiving the best education possible. But none of these efforts should be made in a vacuum. It's important to know exactly where educational problems lie and to target them specifically.

Don't treat only the symptoms; treat the root causes. (Place a strong emphasis on early learning.)

As a former teacher (and hopefully I'm still a teacher in some ways), I have great empathy for people in education and a lot of interest in how to improve it. Escambia County has a history of low graduation rates. In 2014, the high school graduation rate was 66 percent. In reviewing our dashboard, we noticed our kindergarten readiness rate was *also* 66 percent. What a coincidence…or was it? Through our research at the Studer Community Institute, we discovered that no, the two identical numbers were no coincidence.

As it turns out, early childhood learning is strongly linked to brain development. The better the brain development the more prepared children are for kindergarten. And when they enter school prepared to learn, they have a much better chance of completing their education and going on to become productive and thriving citizens. That means communities that want a high graduation rate must take action not when kids are in high school or even elementary or middle schools, but practically from the time they're born. This type of approach is also better for teachers. When a child is unprepared for kindergarten (or any grade for that matter), they are not only more difficult to teach, but they also make it harder for the teacher to teach the rest of the class.

As mentioned earlier, Pensacola sought out experts to help us understand issues in early learning. This led us to Dr. Dana Suskind, who is a cochlear implant surgeon at the University of Chicago Medicine Comer Children's Hospital. Dr. Suskind has conducted important research about the impact of learning very early in life. Her book, *Thirty Million Words: Building a Child's Brain*, reveals that children who hear more words in infancy are better prepared when they enter school. (This does *not* mean words heard on TV, but words spoken to them by other human beings.)

So we brought Dr. Suskind to Pensacola and had her look at our community and talk about what we could do. She told us that 85 percent of all brain development happens in the first three years of life. To drill down to the root cause of our low high school graduation rates, we needed to reach our at-risk kids early on. In fact, we realized that to help Pensacola's children reach their full potential, we needed to start doing brain intervention from birth.

If you think about it, this timing makes perfect sense. When a baby is born, parents get all sorts of training in the hospital. They are taught how to feed and bathe the baby, when the umbilical cord is going to fall off, how to maximize breastfeeding, etc. So this also seems like the perfect time to educate parents on the importance of early brain development and how it impacts their child's future.

We partnered with the University of Chicago and formed a pilot program to make sure every mother who gave birth in one of the three hospitals in Escambia County gets an early intervention. That's 5,000 births a year. These hospitals—Baptist, Sacred Heart, and West Florida—distribute materials developed from the Thirty Million Words Initiative designed to help new parents work more words into their interactions with their babies and young children.

Early results are promising. We're seeing that once parents learn how important it is to talk to their child they *will* make an effort to do it. Because they love their child, they can't not do it. Parents vary in age, education, race, and income, but what they *don't* vary in is the desire for their child to be successful.

This is an especially important message to share at a time when there are so many distractions for parents, and busy lives might keep them from engaging with their children.

There is no way to predict how successful this effort will be over time. But we owe it to our children and our community to act now. One of my favorite sayings is, "The best time to plant a tree is 20 years ago; the second best time is today." Sometimes we have to take action just because it makes sense and trust that results will come in the long term. However, there are some short-term wins too. Every parent who is taught how to build a child's brain becomes a better parent.

America's First Early Learning City

In Pensacola we believe so strongly in the importance of building brains that we are on track to become America's first Early Learning City.™ (In fact, we've trademarked this phrase.) Our goal is to move our kindergarten readiness score to the best in the state. The goal is for all parts of the community—healthcare, public schools, businesses, the media, etc.—to work as one to make sure every child is ready for kindergarten.

One part of our strategy is to use visuals to support early learning. For example, the Bodacious Brew Thru, a coffee shop in downtown Pensacola, features an outdoor area designed to stimulate children's cognitive development. The early childhood learning playground features a wooden log course decorated with letters and numbers, a sidewalk chalk station, butterfly-friendly plants, and more.

We wanted to get the community involved in our efforts, so SCI issued a "Be the Bulb" early learning challenge. Some great suggestions came out of this. One was an early learning bus that would be converted to bring educational, health, and wellness resources to small children in communities with the most need. Another idea was pop-up early learning fairs designed to bring fair-themed educational games to community centers, churches, preschools, and elementary schools. On-site screenings would yield results to be used in tailored follow-up to help families track their child's development physically and academically.

We are still in the early stages of these efforts. But we have people thinking about what an Early Learning City might look like. And eventually we'd like to share our model with other communities across America.

The Voluntary Prekindergarten Program

Prekindergarten is also a big part of Pensacola's focus on early learning.

In Florida we have a statewide voluntary prekindergarten (VPK) program. Designed to help prepare children for school socially, emotionally, and academically, it's available free for all four-year-olds in our state. Locally, VPK is managed by the Early Learning Coalition (ELC), which is led by Bruce Watson. Classrooms are hosted in private childcare centers, church-based centers, public and private schools, and Head Start facilities.

In our community, we've found if a child goes to voluntary prekindergarten, there's an 80 percent chance that they will be ready for kindergarten. Data from the state says 50 percent of children who don't attend VPK in Escambia are kindergarten-ready.

The ELC also works with multiple early-education providers like childcare centers, Head Start, family childcare homes, and faith-based providers. All childcare providers are ranked by the coalition on a star rating system that shows parents which ones do the best job at preparing their children for kindergarten.

The connection between early learning and long-term success is clear. When communities get behind these kinds of programs, it ensures that our children have the best possible start in school. This in turn makes it more likely that they will graduate high school and move on to successful lives.

Don't *just* focus on college-bound kids.

Four-year degrees and graduate degrees are important for many jobs. Yet college isn't for everyone. In fact, 60 percent of the jobs in the future won't require a traditional college degree. Plus tuition costs are rising higher and higher. When we see the amount of debt so many young people are burdened with upon graduation, we have to acknowledge that the investment in college isn't always the right one for every student. We've got to be more creative in what we consider education.

It's exciting that more and more universities are now offering certificate programs, many of them accessible online. More and more emphasis is being placed on technical training and apprenticeships. If these trends continue, they'll give more of our kids a way to make a solid living and help provide a workforce for local jobs.

All that being said, we need to work hard to make our public school systems the best they can be. They are an important part of a community's culture and, as mentioned earlier, create the kind of workforce that attracts investors. As we'll discuss in the Attracting Investment chapter, Janesville, WI, has an incredible graduation rate of 93 percent, and it was this strong education system, along with its background as a General Motors city, that convinced Dollar General to put its logistics center there.

Developing Young Leaders

Leadership is more than a business skill; it's a life skill. Teaching young people the fundamentals of leadership helps them build habits that will serve them for a lifetime. It empowers them to solve problems and creates a sense of confidence that they can make the world a better place (and this starts in their own community). When kids learn early that they can make a difference, they will be more motivated to take action.

Every community has a responsibility to help their kids become good leaders. They are our future and we must prepare them. Grooming kids to be leaders can no longer be accidental. The key is to start early and be consistent. It's important that our schools find a way to cultivate and teach these skills. We need to set kids up to become lifelong leaders in the community as well as in the professional world.

A few years back, I spoke at a Student Government Association in Northwest Florida. I asked about their leadership curriculum and realized that they didn't have a standardized one that all the schools could use. This led to the Studer Foundation creating a $50,000 grant that allowed teachers to get together more regularly to develop one. The teachers worked closely with students to get ideas for what they wanted to see in a leadership curriculum. Together, they developed a leadership training program they called Quintessentials.

Students who take this year-long course get the advantage of gaining valuable leadership skills early on. These are skills that are not normally taught in an academic setting: how to practice service leadership, how to set goals and develop a plan for achieving them, how to communicate in a way that gets results, how to resolve conflicts, how to run a good meeting, how to self-assess, how to effectively manage time, how to create an emotional bank account, how to be interested vs. interesting, how to become an influencer, etc. Incidentally, these are the very same skills we used to teach managers of healthcare systems.

What's more, this course makes students more civic-minded. As part of the curriculum, they must complete a service project that benefits their community.

Three years later, the Quintessentials program is still going strong. In fact, teachers in any school system across the nation can download the curriculum for free from our website at https://studeri.org/building-a-vibrant-community.

It is my hope that other communities will replicate this very successful program in their own school systems. It's a wonderful way to give young people real-world experience and equip them with the skill set they will need in the future.

Teach students the skillset of the future.

As technology ushers in the age of automation, many jobs that people have always performed will be taken over by smart robots. That's why the vital job skills of the future will be those no machine can perform—those involving creativity, innovation, problem solving, and emotional intelligence.

Plus, as problems get more complex, teamwork will be more important than ever. No single individual is likely to have all the answers. Workers will need to be able to communicate, connect, and collaborate. Many of the jobs in the future will require that workers quiet their egos, manage their thinking and emotions, and learn to be better listeners.

Here are just a few of the skills that will be valued in the future:

- Humility: Humility doesn't mean being submissive. It means controlling the ego and avoiding being defensive or self-centered. It means admitting that you don't have all the answers and are willing to ask questions, listen to other points of view, and suspend judgment.

- Presence: Modern life teaches us to be reactive and perform quickly, but when people live fully in the moment, they are better listeners and stay in control of their emotions.

- Courage: Fear of failure will be very limiting in the future. In order to excel, we must bravely enter unknown territory and be willing to fail.

- Connection: Our success in the future will depend on our ability to relate to, have compassion for, and emotionally connect with other people.

It's important that our schools find a way to cultivate and teach these skills. We need to set kids up to become lifelong learners, teach them how to work in teams and relate to others, and, rather than memorizing and reciting facts, to think critically, take risks, and challenge assumptions.

Establish or grow a university presence in the community.

In Pensacola, we are very lucky to have great educational options that are continually growing. Our local university, the University of West Florida, was stuck at 10,000 students for years. Current President Martha Saunders and past President Dr. Judith Bense set those "big, hairy, audacious goals," or BHAGs, as James Collins talks about, and now our university has 13,000 people.

We also are fortunate to have Pensacola State College, which has grown from a junior college into a program that now offers a variety of different degrees, including a very strong nursing program. Pensacola Christian College is yet another strong educational option in our area.

In Pensacola, having a college in our own community connects us back to our original mission, which is to keep our children in Pensacola. Even if they don't have a university located in the area, communities can still partner with other colleges to create a local branch, so students can seek higher education close to home.

Having a local college presence benefits the community in a variety of ways. For instance:

Universities boost economic growth. They boost innovation with businesses in the area. In addition, they often purchase goods and services from the region, as well as create economic activity for local businesses. They also increase property values. For a city, a university presence creates higher property taxes.

It gives local businesses more access to talent. It greatly increases the supply of skilled graduates for local businesses. For some companies, the *why* is keeping more talent at home. Students often end up working within 50 to 100 miles of the university they attended.

It provides more opportunity for internships. It's good when people can work and learn in the same community. After graduation they are likely to get hired by the company that provided the internship. Again, this is a good way to keep talent in the community.

It allows you to sponsor scholarships that keep young talent at home. We created a Pensacola Pledge Program that provides scholarships to high school graduates who live in Escambia County to attend either the University of West Florida (UWF) or Pensacola State College. This idea originally came from Kalamazoo, MI. A high percentage of college students end up locating near the school they graduate from, so this program is another step to encourage young talent to stay near home. (A similar program was also initiated between Janesville, WI, and the University of Wisconsin-Whitewater.) This also has the added benefit of keeping our local colleges and universities healthy by keeping enrollment strong.

This is such an exciting time for education. As the way we live and work transforms, the way we teach our young people—in fact, people of all ages—will have to transform too. It's happening now and it will continue to happen. That's why communities need to make education a priority. When we enrich the minds of our greatest resource—our citizens—we create a brighter, richer, more vibrant future for everyone.

CHAPTER 12

The Vital Role of Healthcare Providers

If there's one type of organization in any community that touches every citizen, it's the local healthcare providers. People have babies there, regularly see the physicians who work there, have surgery there, and visit sick family members there. So if any type of organization should be a major part of building a vibrant community, it's them.

A vibrant community needs strong healthcare providers, and strong healthcare providers need a vibrant community. It's a mutually beneficial relationship.

Why does a community benefit from strong healthcare providers? There are several reasons. For starters, they tend to be some of the top employers in the community. If they're strong and healthy, they offer good jobs with solid pay and benefits. This helps keep the local economy strong.

Also, it's important that residents have access to good primary care and specialists. They don't have to travel far to get good care. This keeps money in the community. If you have to travel to see a specialist, money is infused into their economy instead.

Good companies will use a strong healthcare system as a magnet to attract talent. This is a big plus for people moving there. When people are looking to move to an area, they look closely at the healthcare providers. It's part of how they judge the well-roundedness of the community.

Finally, the quality of healthcare provided has a direct impact on the well-being of the community. Healthy citizens create healthy communities.

For all of these reasons, community leaders need to partner with and invest in their local healthcare providers. And the reverse is also true. Healthcare systems should go beyond their role of providing direct patient care and invest in keeping their community healthy and vibrant. Again, this is true for several reasons.

A strong tax base creates a good payer mix. Local healthcare providers are financially impacted by the economic health of their community. If the community is doing well, they win. If not, they lose. All businesses experience ups and downs with the community's ups and downs, but this is even truer for healthcare providers.

Recruitment and retention of physicians is a priority for most healthcare providers. There is a fairly significant doctor shortage in some segments of healthcare and some areas of the country. To attract great physicians, especially in competitive markets, communities need to be vibrant. Physicians and their families are just like everyone else: They want high-performing school systems, a variety of great neighborhoods, and fun and exciting downtowns. Of course, the same holds true for all healthcare professionals.

Healthcare providers are dependent on local talent. In a vibrant city, good local talent doesn't leave. This means you don't have to import nurses, which can be expensive. And working to create a vibrant community is the right thing to do for employees, too. Most radiologists or lab professionals, for example, are trained by the hospital or health system they work in. They go to local schools. They end up living there and raising families. These people aren't as movable.

For instance, a while back, a hospital was looking for a chief nursing officer, and I knew one of the greatest CNOs, who was working at another system. I thought, *This will be the perfect match. This person will thank me for helping her get a CNO job at this larger hospital with more opportunity.* But when I gave her the good news, she said, "I can't move. My mother and father live here, and I'm going to take care of them when they get older."

So yes, healthcare providers owe it to themselves, their employees, and, of course, their patients to help create vibrant, healthy communities. If a healthcare provider is in an area where the payer mix goes south on them, they can't just pick up and move. They have to make the community better. And the good news is, there are plenty of creative ways healthcare providers can get involved.

Over the years there have been healthcare providers that started out in more affluent parts of the community, and those areas later ended up being distressed. Some of them moved to locations with better payer mixes, but many of them, because of the cost of moving and their mission, chose not to move. What's really neat is when healthcare providers don't just think, *How do we wall ourselves in?* but instead they reach out and try to create safety in these distressed neighborhoods. They very aggressively work with the communities to create better neighborhoods.

For instance, Baptist Health Care in Pensacola is very interested in improving the neighborhoods around their community. In 2017, after Chuck Marohn kicked off CivicCon—a speaker series sponsored by Studer Community Institute and the *Pensacola News Journal*—Baptist invited him back right away to speak to their organization. Chuck, the founder and president of Strong Towns, is committed to helping make communities better. His ideas resonated with the healthcare provider, which is deeply aware that they have a symbiotic relationship with their local neighborhoods and want to do all they can to contribute to their well-being.

Healthcare providers across the nation have this mindset. There are lots of stories about providers that create loan programs to help employees pay for homes if they're within a certain geographic distance to the hospital. They might also run clinics in the neighborhoods. There are plenty of out-of-the-box ways healthcare providers can become good neighborhood players. They might make neighborhoods more walkable, expand provider security into the surrounding neighborhoods, and create grants that neighborhood associations can access to help revitalize and improve certain areas.

It's no secret that healthcare has always been a major player in local business communities. Their leaders are active in chambers of commerce, in the United Way, on boards, and in various other leadership capacities. These are all important. Most administrative and medical staff leaders happily give of their time and energy and are deeply engaged in improving the long-term health of their communities.

So, too, are employees at every level. I've spent many years working with healthcare professionals and I know that they are naturally caring, compassionate, and civic-minded people. There is no question in my mind that healthcare attracts a very special type of person.

Besides the immediate neighborhood improvements mentioned earlier, providers partner with their larger communities in various ways. They partner with schools to provide health services (dental screenings, etc.) and to teach kids about healthcare careers. They host health fairs. They build walking trails. They sponsor farmers markets and food banks in low-income communities.

In Pensacola's case, local providers have been instrumental in rolling out our early brain development program. As you'll recall from the Focus on Education chapter, when we were looking for a way to improve our high school graduation rates, we discovered a correlation with our kindergarten readiness rates. Both were at 66 percent. We realized to create an economically healthier community we needed to not only treat the symptoms (poor graduation rates) but also tackle the root cause (the inadequate early brain development that manifested as poor kindergarten readiness).

We researched what's needed for the best early brain development and discovered that a language-rich environment is a critical piece of the puzzle. In fact, 85 percent of the brain is developed in the first three years. By focusing on getting parents to talk more with their young children, we could significantly impact kindergarten readiness and move the needle on our high school graduation rates. And when we explained this to the leaders of our local hospitals, they immediately saw that they could help.

We partnered with the University of Chicago and formed a pilot program to make sure every mother who gave birth in one of the three hospitals in Escambia County gets an early intervention. That's 5,000 births a year. These hospitals—Baptist, Sacred Heart, and West Florida—distribute materials developed from the Thirty Million Words Initiative designed to help new parents work more words into their interactions with their babies and young children.

This is a very doable program and easy to replicate. The impact it has on new mothers is simply amazing. Best of all it's a very low-cost way to help children, parents, and the community as a whole. Not only will healthcare providers that adopt it help make significant strides toward solving a fundamental problem, it's a good way for them to show that they are truly invested in the future of the children in the community.

For more information about the early brain development program, please contact Studer Community Institute at www.studeri.org.

CHAPTER 13

Think Inclusion

We hear a lot about diversity these days. Diversity is valuable because it offers representation to different groups who in the past haven't had an equal voice or a vote. But diversity isn't the only factor that's important in building vibrant communities. To really build a thriving community, inclusion is also important.

Inclusion means giving everyone—racial minorities, women, all sexual orientations, all economic groups, and citizens of all ages—a seat at the table, and *also* giving them an active role in the restoration of the community. It's not enough to elect African American city council members, hire a Muslim employee, or find jobs for high school drop-outs. These are good first steps, but more is needed.

Don't be mistaken: Diversity can provide enormous resources for invigorating communities. But turning it into real inclusion is complicated. Inclusion isn't just something that happens in a community as a byproduct of being diverse; it's something that has to be consciously and intentionally created.

Diversity takes care of the *who* and the *what*. Inclusion takes care of the *how*.

Inclusion benefits a community in many ways.

Inclusion is more than just the right thing to do. It is a vital tool to push a community forward. Here are several ways inclusion helps a community:

Inclusion develops trust. When only one segment of the community is doing well, there is a sense that there are "haves" and "have-nots," and that the game is rigged to create winners at the expense of the losers. Specifically in communities where growth has been stagnant, people are often stuck in the mindset that the pie is only so big. They believe that if someone is getting something, that it's being taken away from someone else. This breeds a culture of competition, when cooperation is really what is needed.

In fact, in some instances, people will say, "If we can't get the contract, I hope an out-of-town company gets it so my competitor doesn't get it." Until these people see the pie grow, they can't believe that it's actually going to get bigger. It's difficult to break through that mindset, but it's really important to get all of these people working on the same team. The best way to do this is to consistently remind everyone what the goal is: to grow the pie, not split it up. A culture of scarcity is replaced with a culture of opportunity.

It attracts new business and young talent. Businesses are more attracted to communities where inclusion is part of their culture. They understand that companies thrive when more voices are heard and that talented young people want to live and work in these communities. An inclusive atmosphere can also help you attract top talent and new business and supercharge economic growth.

It drives innovation. Inclusivity means creating a strong participatory culture, with the active involvement of all members in planning and decision making. New voices, new networks, and different team combinations open up and present new experiences, skills, and perspectives. This really opens the door for growth and innovation, as it provides a fresh look at old problems.

It promotes equality and stability. Inclusion helps combat poverty and inequality. Whether it's intentional or not, when people are excluded from planning conversations and other resources, it's much harder for that group to be upwardly mobile. When all of the business ideas are coming from a small section of the population, growth in the community is disproportionate and unsustainable. In other words, if a community is not intentional about combatting it, the rich get richer and the poor stay poor. Including the whole community in the development process will help focus growth initiatives in poor and disenfranchised areas of the community.

It promotes buy-in. When people feel included, they are more likely to buy into improvement efforts. When citizens feel like the game isn't fair, they are not likely to engage in civil or social participation. They have no real sense of belonging to the community and they feel disenfranchised. This feeling also drives apathy. Not only do they often have more pressing personal concerns (like putting food on the table), they also feel little ownership over the community.

To foster real social progress, all groups must be invested, and believe that the improvements being made will directly benefit them as well as their neighbors. Everyone has to have some stake in the community. When everyone is included in the development and revitalization process, each group takes pride and ownership in the process.

It decreases crime. Inclusivity can also help cut down on crime. When economic opportunities are available, criminal activity decreases. When citizens are part of an inclusive community, they become stakeholders and benefit by keeping it safer. They are more connected with their neighbors and more mindful of community activity. What's more, when they feel included and engaged in the process of governing, they are much more likely to follow the rules.

In short, inclusivity enriches all of our lives. Building an inclusive community leads to a stronger community. Plus, it's just the right thing to do. Everyone should be involved in making decisions that impact a community.

How to Implement Inclusion in Your Community

So, here are some ways to build inclusion in your community to consider:

Do the homework. Learn the history of the community and the people who live there. Find the major groups that make up the community and listen to what they care about. Try to understand their concerns and where they come from. Speak to groups in terms of what their *what* is. In other words, what does each group most care about? Better quality of life? Safe streets? More opportunities for their children? This *what* becomes the "burning platform" that will move them to action. By forging relationships with community leaders, both formal and informal, partnerships are developed that will help in learning more about each group's issues.

Go where the people are. People who feel disenfranchised won't likely show up for community meetings. It's important to meet them where they are.

Local churches and rec centers are great places to bring information and ask for feedback to hear from a variety of people. Spending time with the different groups in the community will help build relationships and also help humanize the issues that matter to them.

Create opportunities for early participation to generate best solutions. It's always best if communities can be inclusive in the early stages of change. Include as many groups as possible in the planning phase and in early conversations. This means more than just having every group represented at the meeting. Give them a voice and a real chance to participate in the process. After all, they know the most about how things will impact their communities, and they are the best source of ideas on how to solve the problems they are facing.

Getting input from all groups will help keep mistakes from being made and provide a much more accurate picture of a situation. Plus, they are much more inclined to help execute the plan when they feel part of the planning process.

Commit to building trust. Expect some skepticism and know that engaging diverse groups isn't going to come easy. Without trust, inclusion is almost impossible. Groups that have been historically disenfranchised are likely to be skeptical about how projects will actually help them. There are going to be times when leadership doesn't have enough credibility to just say "trust me." Skepticism is often the result of history. People who have been let down for decades aren't just going to trust everything someone tells them. Sometimes it has to be put in writing, and there's nothing wrong with that. But over time, by following through on promises, it's possible to build up trust within the community.

Ensure institutions treat everyone equally. Eliminate prejudice in community institutions including schools, law enforcement, etc. Support from these institutions is crucial. Engage their leaders in the inclusion efforts and show them how they can benefit from valuing and including all of the major groups. It's also important that these institutions are responsive to feedback from the community.

Create gathering places for all groups to mingle. Develop interactive and accessible community spaces where people can gather. These spaces encourage integration and cooperation between people and organizations in the community, which in turn feeds back into a rise in public and private investment in the social and economic well-being of the community. A vibrant downtown that has been well programmed serves this purpose well.

Foster inclusion with children. Once you capture the young people and teach them the value of inclusion, they'll grow up with these attitudes. This helps make inclusivity a real part of the community's values over time.

Celebrate successful collective action (no matter how small). Celebrate and acknowledge the smallest accomplishments publicly. This is a really good investment of time and resources. It not only lets people know that you're paying attention, but also makes it more likely that this behavior will be repeated.

How a Promise to the Community Created a Win-Win for Pensacola

Economic inequality is often a source of major divide between groups in communities. In Pensacola, we were keenly aware that we had to empower disadvantaged communities to create their own economic success to help bridge this gap. However, the dots between the Community Maritime Park Project and economic activity had to be connected.

Going into the park project, I felt I had a lot of credibility with minority groups in the community. As the president of Baptist Hospital in Pensacola, which was a large minority employer in the area, I had worked hard to build a culture of inclusion. I thought I was going into the project with a large emotional bank account. While trying to rally support for the project, I went to talk to many minority groups. I was hoping that they would support the project because it would bring new jobs to the area. While some were supportive, others had seen projects like this in the past, and didn't believe the benefits would really flow to them. They wanted specifics; they wanted us to be intentional about including them.

In talking with them, the conversation went something like this:

Group: "How many of these new jobs are going to be held by minorities?"

Quint: "Given that minorities make up about 30 percent of the population, it would be fair for them to hold at least 30 percent of the jobs."

Group: "Do you really believe that is going to happen?"

Quint: "Yeah, I believe that."

Group: "Can we trust you?"

Quint: "Yeah, you can trust me."

Group: "What happens if we don't trust you? If you believe it so much, why not put it in writing?"

Quint: "Okay, help me put it in writing."

The Covenant for the Community Is Born

We sat down and created something we called the Covenant for the Community. This was an agreement that spells out specific inclusion and hiring goals for contractors working on building projects. (See Appendix A for full copy of the covenant.) This would not only create jobs in the community, but it would keep the dollars circulating there.

Initially, there was some pushback from contractors. They said, "We can't hit those numbers. We've never hit those numbers before." While these were lofty goals, it was important that they put in a good faith effort. As a part of the covenant, we outlined exactly what this looked like in order to eliminate any confusion, including very specific goals. We created a situation where the firms we worked with either had to hit these numbers or work to prove that it was impossible. Everyone involved really had to work hard in order to make it happen, but we hit the numbers on the first construction project. As time went on, it got easier to hit the numbers. The population was available and ready to work, and contractors were very serious about making this happen.

In many cases we were able to ask large firms we had worked with in the past to pair with small, locally owned firms, including many that were owned by minorities. For some of these smaller local companies, we needed to provide some cash up front to purchase equipment, find employees, and help fund other resources. There were also times when we had to help with cash flow throughout the project. Because these were small firms, they were really working on very thin margins, which is hard to do on some of these big projects.

The Covenant for the Community helps create sustainable growth.

The support that was provided along the way helped the larger firms meet the inclusion goals. It also helped the smaller firms get some on-the-job training and experience and the opportunity to work on projects they would never have gotten to otherwise. General contractors met and worked with companies and employees they likely would not normally be exposed to. These relationships carried over to other projects and gave many local people chances to keep working. This helped build up the population of skilled tradespeople in the area.

With each project, it got easier and easier. Developing and using these local firms really pays off in the long run. It may take more time, and they may require more support, but these dollars get pumped back into the local economy.

When the covenant was first created as part of the Community Maritime Park Project, public money was funding the construction efforts. Studer Properties uses the covenant for all private development projects. For a $16-million office building, we set the minority workers goal to 30 percent and reached 40 percent. For a $52-million apartment complex (Southtowne), minorities made up 51 percent of the labor force, and for the $14.4-million mixed-use office building next to it, the minority participation is at 38 percent.

Some projects focus inclusion efforts around hiring minority-owned companies. However, it's crucial to make sure you are truly creating jobs and developing workforce skills for the minority employees in the community. This is where you can see real economic impact.

While this has had a very positive impact on poverty, we still have a long way to go. The Covenant for the Community is just a start. Creating the document and enforcing it showed everyone we were serious about including minorities in the revitalization efforts. The document also created a lot of transparency and accountability, which was badly needed. It helped foster trust and develop relationships, which are vital parts of inclusion.

Economic inclusion takes more than writing a check.

Carefully directing development projects is a great way to incubate small business, as well as work toward real economic inclusion, but it's also important to make progress in other sectors of the economy. When thinking about how you foster economic opportunity, look past simply providing funding. We learned how important it is to provide the additional support necessary to get those crucial early businesses off the ground. Things like providing coaching and affordable office space go a long way.

For example, in Pensacola there was an African American chef named Cecil Johnson who ran a small restaurant business. We wanted to help him grow his restaurant into a real destination and move to a central downtown location. Just giving him a loan to rent a new building wouldn't be enough. We purchased all the equipment, renovated the building, including two upstairs apartments, and created a lease with rent that moved up and down based on revenue. Due to Cecil's hard work and great food, the Five Sisters Blues Café in Pensacola's historic black district was a hit.

These stories are a real inspiration to others in the community. People see that success is possible, and they start to work harder for it themselves. Plus, these early success stories become community leaders that help inspire and coach others to follow in their footsteps. Lumon May, for example, owned one of the local minority-owned construction companies we worked with through the Covenant for the Community. He went on to become one of the five elected commissioners for Escambia County.

Building inclusive communities is not easy. It happens at multiple levels: institutions, cultural groups, individuals. You can't expect to see results happen overnight. Transforming attitudes and behaviors takes time and patience, but it is worth the effort.

CHAPTER 14

Capture the Youth

Young people are some of the most valuable assets in building a vibrant community. Think about the word "vibrant." It refers to the state of being filled with energy, enthusiasm, and vitality. Youth *is* vibrancy. Young people naturally have the spirit we want to impart to our community, so it stands to reason that we should look to them to help shape and build it.

Getting young people involved in your efforts builds the city's "bench." Be deliberate and proactive about doing this. If not, it's easy for the old guard to keep making all the decisions. Before you know it, young people disengage, and meaningful change will happen slowly, if at all.

Involving young people will help a community make better decisions. Remember, the best decisions come from diverse groups of people. Plus, if young people get involved, it's more likely that people from all walks of life will be part of the decision-making process. Young people are inclusive and tolerant by nature. They tend to see past race and gender.

Recruiting young people helps them see the value of giving back to the community. Get to them early, and they'll become lifelong civic-minded citizens. It develops a sense of citizenship and stewardship, which is vital in a vibrant community.

It makes community issues that they would otherwise see only in the news—"Referendum 12 passed last night after a tough battle"—real to them. They get to see the evolution of how decisions come to be made.

It will also help them enhance skill sets like leadership, communication, and organizational skills. These are incredibly valuable in the marketplace. Plus, they will learn the art of negotiation and compromise. For example, they will learn that it's okay to change your mind after you get more info. This happens all the time in business and in government (or at least it should).

Don't wait for the youth to get involved on their own, but actively engage them. Young people may be hesitant to get involved if we don't actively seek them out. I've found that some young people are a little timid. They don't want to step on toes. They're fearful that they might not have the skill set to do it or they may not have the initial interest. Some will wait for the baton to be handed down to them from more senior people in the community. My message is always, "Don't wait for the baton to be handed down to you. Grab the baton and run with it." Most people are just glad that somebody else is taking it off their hands!

The good news is it's just not that hard to get young people involved. Often, it's just a matter of asking. They have a vested interest already. They want to live and work in their community. They don't want to watch their friends leave town because there are no jobs.

Also, young people are idealistic. They want to be part of something great and part of a solution. They want to throw their arms around a project or cause. They want to be part of a movement, and it's even better if they can get in on the front end.

Young people played a huge part in Pensacola's revitalization. Many of them saw their friends leaving town, not because they really wanted to leave, but because they were forced to leave. They wished they could stay but they couldn't find opportunity. So this resulted in a groundswell of young people who were motivated to change things. A couple of young leaders, John Hosman and Jason Crawford, and also an individual named Rick Outzen, who ran an independent newspaper, started asking, "What can we do to help move the community forward?"

A group called the Pensacola Young Professionals (PYP) got together and started forming subcommittees and really looking for solutions. They saw that the Community Maritime Park Initiative had a lot of potential in moving Pensacola forward. It was something they could really put their arms around. And so they became really instrumental in getting the message out and getting people engaged. They really did the legwork, pounded the pavement, and connected with a lot of citizens on a personal level.

As we were trying to determine what metrics we should focus on to keep the community progressing, the PYP got involved. They took over the Pensacola Quality of Life Survey, which was done by Mason-Dixon Polling & Research. Having them manage this survey was a tremendous win, because it gave them a sense of accomplishment and really gelled them together as a group. And it also developed in them a passion for the community. Once they started getting involved in local issues, they became owners, not renters.

The Pensacola Young Professionals became a vital arm for moving their community forward. They made sure young people had a voice in the revitalization of Pensacola. But also, their work became a training ground that got them ready for other things. People who are below the age of 30 or so might not be ready to serve on a board or to take on some other major position in the community. But by working with the PYP, they learned lessons and gained confidence in how to pull off something big. They became leaders among the leaders.

Looking back now, ten years later, I see that many of these individuals are now in leadership positions in the community. A lot of them are running their own businesses. So their experience with PYP set the stage for the future. This success can easily be duplicated in almost any community.

Ken Ford, who is founder and CEO of the Florida Institute for Human & Machine Cognition (IHMC)—and who was inducted into the Florida Inventors Hall of Fame in November 2017—also brought a lot of young people to Pensacola. He was one of the early drivers for revitalizing the community because he needed to attract world-class talent to the institute. He was instrumental in bringing experts like Jim Clifton and Ray Gindroz to town to help us figure out how to create the kind of downtown where young people want to work, live, and play.

Dr. Ford talked to me about his conversations with young people in making the decision to build IHMC in Pensacola. Basically, he convinced them they were on the cusp of something great. He helped them see that Pensacola was large enough that IHMC could attract the right people but small enough that they could make a big difference in the community and local economy. This was something they wouldn't be able to do in a big city.

He also got them excited about buying old historic houses and fixing them up. This created in them a tremendous feeling of pride and a sense of belonging to a community that they had helped build. They became committed and deeply engaged residents.

So that's how Pensacola captured the youth. Other communities can do similar things to replicate our success. What these things are will, of course, vary based on their unique needs and circumstances. But here are a few suggestions that may help.

Getting Young People Involved in Your Community

First thing to remember: Young people are very different from middle-aged and older people. Try to understand how and why, and learn to appreciate their differences. Millennials simply want a different way of life. So they will need to be reached in different ways. A few suggestions:

Find the influencers and connectors. Grab them right away and get them involved. They will attract others. (In Pensacola this was PYP. What similar group might exist in your town? If there isn't such a group, it might be time to create one.)

Don't micromanage them. Young people need to feel empowered. Give them a project and let them make it their own. Their solutions might be different and nontraditional, but it doesn't mean they're wrong.

Emphasize the business skills they'll be learning. Help them connect the dots that these skills will be valuable in their career. Invite them to educational events where they can learn these skills. (For example, in Pensacola, Studer Community Institute holds monthly workforce development workshops, small business roundtables, and our annual business conference, EntreCon.)

Remember that social media is their medium. Reach out to them via platforms like Twitter, Facebook, Instagram, and Meetup.

Meet in fun venues. Microbreweries and coffee shops are always good options. They tend to avoid the traditional conference room-style meetings.

Reward and recognize their efforts often. This could mean anything from sending a thank-you letter to public recognition to a professional reference or recommendation. Positive reinforcement will keep young people coming back and doing their best work.

Once young people initially get engaged, they start getting engaged on a lot of other levels. This really promotes business development, civic engagement, and volunteerism. Getting young people enthusiastic about what happens in the community is truly an investment in the future—one that will pay off in all sorts of ways, now and later on.

CHAPTER 15

Attracting Investment

Every great community begins with great ideas. However, until those ideas are put into action, they don't create change. Action requires human capital and financial investment. Communities have to position themselves to attract investors.

Of course, the best kind of investment is internal investment. Potential investors who live and work in a community care deeply about that community. They have an emotional attachment that doesn't exist with those from the outside. Internal investors know they may not get the maximum ROI in terms of dollars. That's okay with them: Their real ROI is the healthier, more vibrant community that results from their investment.

Communities should do everything they can to find, engage, and nurture these internal investors. Share ideas with them. Constantly connect back to the *why*—"We're doing this so we can create a community where our children and grandchildren will be able to find fulfilling work and live great lives"—and invite their feedback. Reward and recognize them for their efforts.

Make these internal investors your priority—but know that outside investors can also be extremely valuable in building vibrant communities. That's what this chapter is about.

All that said, private investment must lead the way. As we've already discussed, no community can depend on the government to drive growth long term. For one thing, government officials probably don't have the budget to help fund investments. And even if they could, they come and go with election cycles, so they couldn't possibly maintain continuity on big projects.

It's time to forget the old "if you build it they will come" approach. Communities have tried this for years and are finding it doesn't work. Vibrant communities must develop organically. Once private investment gets the ball rolling, then public investment and infrastructure can follow.

So what's the best way to attract investment? There is no single answer, but we have found that the process is both a science and an art. The "science" part is the metrics and dashboard. (See the Creating a Tailored Approach for Your City chapter for a refresher.) Providing businesses and investors with good, concise information about relevant factors—economic performance, well-being of the population, and where entrepreneurs are located, for example—will be what attracts investment. So pay close attention to what is being reported and how it is being presented.

The "art" part is the compelling story that is built around that data. For example, does the community have a high graduation rate? Are there a lot of Millennials? These are the kinds of data points that can be used to showcase a community's advantages.

There may also be other advantages that don't necessarily show up on a dashboard. Is there a great downtown? A great university? Is the community known for arts and culture? Is the cost of living affordable? Great! Be sure to focus on these selling points.

Know the city's culture. How is the city described by people on the outside looking in? How do residents feel about themselves? Figure out how to sum up the city's culture and create sort of an elevator speech around it. Then repeat this message again and again. Talk to people about "managing up" the community to everyone they meet. Managing the messaging around culture is an important part of showcasing a community to investors.

Every community has something to offer the right investor.

Don't assume every company is looking for a big city. They're not. They're looking for a city that's the right size for their needs. While being a smaller city might make it harder to attract investment in some cases, it can also be an advantage. Workers and businesses simply want to go somewhere that feels relevant and vibrant.

Ken Ford, who is founder and CEO of the Florida Institute for Human & Machine Cognition, brought his organization to Pensacola because it wasn't a huge city. He felt it was the perfect size: big enough to attract the right people, yet small enough that IHMC would make a big impact on the community and in the local economy.

Sometimes communities overlook things that are truly unique about themselves. This is one reason it's so important to have a dashboard. Not only does it help leaders make decisions on facts rather than opinions, showcase what needs fixing, and help connect seemingly unconnected dots, it also reveals a city's greatest assets. Without a dashboard, a city might miss out on great solutions for attracting investors.

Janesville, WI, has this really cool program called Bright Spots. They send teachers and principals to other cities in the U.S. to harvest good ideas, bring them back home, and implement them. I was in Janesville for the ten-year anniversary of Bright Spots, and during the celebration they happened to share their school system's high school graduation rate. It had gone from what was a fairly high rate already to 93 percent.

So I'm sitting there thinking, *Wow!* I travel the country and see a lot of different communities and a lot of school systems, and there's no question that's an exceptional high school graduation rate. As I complimented the school district, I felt that they were taking all of their hard work for granted. Compared with other communities, Janesville's graduation rate was truly impressive.

I was thinking about a billboard I had just seen on the interstate that advertised Janesville's shovel-ready land. Well, almost any town can say that. It's not a big deal anymore. A city has to have shovel-ready land just to get in the game. What *is* unusual, and what's the hardest thing for businesses to find right now, is talent. So I said, "If I were you guys, I'd change my billboards. I'd say Janesville is a talent-ready community."

The moral is that the things taken for granted could actually be a powerful competitive advantage for your community. At times it is so easy to focus on what's not going well, and what's missed are the many positive outcomes. Take time to pause and enjoy the successes.

Also, don't assume every company is looking for a lot of people with advanced degrees. In many cases, they are looking for an engaged, productive workforce that wants to build a career with a company. Janesville illustrates this point as well.

Janesville lost the General Motors plant back in 2009. So now they have this incredible culture that a lot of towns don't. They have all these workers who have proven they could do the hard work at GM. And so when Dollar General was looking for a place to put a logistics center that needed 500 employees, they were attracted to Janesville. They could find shovel-ready land anywhere. What they couldn't find just anywhere was the kind of workforce Janesville could offer. It was just part of the fabric of their community.

Certainly, Janesville's good high schools helped create this culture. It's not like Dollar General was saying, "We want 500 college graduates." What they said was, "We want 500 people with good attitudes who could work hard and learn." Because Janesville had invested in their talent, they could provide that incredibly valuable resource. Dollar General got some land the city wasn't going to use anyway, but the real incentive was the talent. Now Janesville suddenly has 500 citizens with decent wages and benefits.

The Janesville story is a great example of what being talent-ready looks like. They just had to learn how to communicate that.

A Few Ways to Attract Investors

There are many things leaders can do to attract investors, both from outside and inside the community. Here are a few of them.

Keep young talent from leaving. Businesses want to invest in cities with a young workforce. This is why it's so important to create a vibrant downtown. Young people want to be able to work, live, and play in the same location. They like lots of great restaurants, a dynamic nightlife, and cool places to live. They like river walks, thriving arts districts, and street musicians. Creating a great place to live will attract young people to a city and keep them there.

Elect and appoint leaders who put the community first. They should be willing to listen to new ideas and make it easy and comfortable for people to do business there. That means ensuring that all guidelines, codes, and zoning rules make sense and are clearly spelled out and enforced. It means leaders are easily accessible and available to answer questions. (Remember, there are a lot of details involved in planning and developing, and decisions need to be made quickly and efficiently and in the right sequence.) Above all, it means there is lots of transparency and everyone is treated fairly.

Commit to a "zero tolerance" policy for shadow deals. A shadow deal is exactly what it sounds like. It's a business transaction (especially one involving the government) in which everybody doesn't have a fair chance to participate, or one in which motivations are hidden.

One example might be a building that's sold to someone who had the "inside track." The building is in trouble, and the buyer knows that because he is on the board of directors at the bank. His insider knowledge gives him an unfair advantage. Another example is a public official who is really pushing for a project because a friend of his owns a company that would garner work from it. Yet he hides his real motivation, and that makes it a shadow deal.

In healthy communities, shadow deals have to be disrupted. Force all aspects of the transaction into the light of day. Everyone needs to agree to the rules ahead of time. Procedures need to be followed to the letter. Everyone needs to have a chance to bid. And if someone might benefit from a deal being proposed, it needs to be disclosed. It's fine to have a vested interest in a deal; just disclose it so people can make decisions with all the information.

Fairness and transparency create an environment of trust, and that attracts investors. Get and keep a reputation of doing business fairly.

Make workforce development a priority. Do everything possible to offer training and support for the business community. When trying to attract new business to the city, it's important to provide some resources around workforce development. Getting a new business started is one thing. Sustaining it is quite another. This is why in Pensacola, Studer Community Institute offers training and development sessions and small business roundtables for owners. It's why we encourage mentoring. And it's why we hold EntreCon, our annual business conference that provides a way for local entrepreneurs, professionals, and leaders to come together, learn from experts on their most pressing problems, and learn from each other.

If at all possible, establish or grow a university presence in the community. This is a big part of creating an educated population. Even if there isn't currently a university in town, the community can still partner with other colleges to create a local branch, so students can seek higher education closer to home. Universities are good for economic growth; they give local businesses more access to talent, and they provide opportunity for internships and scholarships. They can even partner with companies to develop specific training programs. They also increase property values.

Focus on culture. Show businesses that the city can do more than help them make a profit. Create a city culture that they want to be a part of. (This environment will help them attract talent, too.) Cultivating a collaborative, genuinely thriving and appealing community fuels hope and optimism. A creative community is part of the mix. Today's entrepreneurs aren't really socialites who hang out in private clubs. They are excited and inspired by places bustling with activity—where they can both live and socialize. Foster a population of artists and visionaries.

Find ways to help start-ups get access to capital. Asheville, NC, does a really good job with investing in small businesses and start-ups. They have Mountain BizWorks, which is a one-stop shop for small businesses looking to grow their existing business or create start-ups in the Asheville area. This entrepreneurship initiative matches qualifying candidates with the resources needed to make their ventures successful. Their model is based on an approach they call "lending and learning." This means helping small businesses get access to capital through microlending, but also providing the additional resources to help them be successful. Resources include things like peer coaching, entrepreneurship networking events, and even business classes through the local community college. They focus on companies that can provide local jobs that would have a hard time securing funding through banks or other traditional sources. To date, they've helped start 1,500 small businesses in the Asheville community, including many minority-owned companies.

We actually learned a lot from talking to Asheville leaders. They taught us that entrepreneurs need more than a space; they might need a little help. And so they help by providing funds for start-up costs like equipment and building renovations and creating leases that move up and down based on revenue. We actually used this technique to help Cecil Johnson open the Five Sisters Blues Café in Pensacola's historic black district. It is a huge success. (See The Pensacola Story chapter for more detail.)

Focus on local growth and reinvestment, too. Not all investment is outside investment. Pay attention to the companies that are already doing well in the community and keep them there! Don't always be recruiting the new. It's easier to join a winning team! Especially nurture those companies that get revenue from outside the community. Ask what their needs are and do everything possible to meet them.

Get some wealth off the sidelines. Community philanthropy is a really important source of investment. This is all about mobilizing capital with the goal of improving citizens' lives. Seek out possible sources of benevolent wealth and approach them about investing in the community. These early investors provide cover for those investors who follow later. It's true that they might make more money other places, but there are other forms of ROI. The satisfaction of helping to build a vibrant community is its own reward.

Build and showcase some small wins. Investment follows investment. Success breeds success, just like failure breeds failure. Capitalizing on some early small wins will help get local private investors interested. If they see that previous efforts have worked, they'll be excited about the results, and they'll want more of the same. In Pensacola two of our small wins were opening the Bodacious Olive store and doing a big renovation on Jewelers Trade Shop. These really impressed the community and inspired other investors. See The Pensacola Story chapter and the Best Odds for Success chapter to learn more about small wins.

Diversify, diversify, diversify. It's easy to have a little success in one area and then focus on that area too much. Healthy economies are based on more than just tourism or just manufacturing or just banking. They need diversity to thrive. So enjoy the successes, but don't get too complacent and keep trying to replicate the same types of businesses over and over.

Bubba Watson and the "Pebble in the Pond" Effect

Once investment gets rolling, the right people will be attracted, and these people will attract more of the right people, and this will result in more investment. It all works organically. Like the ripples caused by a pebble tossed in a pond, growth keeps expanding and creating new momentum.

In Pensacola, one of those ripples was golf professional Bubba Watson and his wife, Angie Watson. I was recently blessed, as chairman of Sacred Heart Health System's Board of Directors, to introduce this couple to speak. They had just given $2.1 million to the Studer Family Children's Hospital. Anyway, they got up to speak. Bubba talked about coming back home to Pensacola, where he had family, and how much it meant to him to be back. Angie discussed how comfortable she felt when she got to Pensacola.

Previously, the couple had lived in Orlando. But when they were here visiting, they loved the revitalization that was going on and they felt they might want to live here. And so they moved to Pensacola.

By attracting the Watsons back home, we attracted more than a celebrity golf pro and a wonderful ex-WNBA player (Angie), and their two great children, Caleb and Dakota. We also brought investors. Bubba and Angie not only came back to our community, but they invested in businesses: a baseball team, a candy store, apartments, an office building, and a car dealership.

By the way, Angie Watson was a big win for the community. She is a very bright lady. She sits on a hospital board and is very active in her church and in the community.

Finally, we attracted philanthropy. If Bubba and Angie weren't living in town, I can't guarantee the $2.1 million donation would've come to this area.

And of course, Bubba's and Angie's presence and all their generosity may well end up attracting more of the same.

This is the best kind of investment because it happens organically. It doesn't need to be forced. Too many communities think only of incentives when they think of attracting investments. There is nothing wrong with incentives, but they are only one piece of the puzzle. And they need to be handled the right way.

Thoughtfully Manage Incentives

Nearly every state and local economic development plan includes incentives. In an effort to encourage businesses to create or retain jobs and make investments, governments spend billions of dollars every year on tax credits, deductions, or exemptions. But while these incentives can be a powerful tool for boosting economic development, they aren't always designed or managed well—and they end up not creating the intended results. As a result, they have become controversial over the years.

Some of these incentives focus on bringing large outside companies into a community in order to create jobs. While sometimes incentives are overused, sometimes they *are* the right choice. My experience has been that with a thoughtful approach and lots of care to make the right decisions for the community, one can achieve good results with incentives.

The problem is that local governments sometimes agree to incentives too quickly without knowing just how effective they are. Be sure an incentive makes financial sense once the impact of tax breaks on school districts and infrastructure, the positive impact of job creation, anticipated future property tax values, and so forth is factored in.

To make sure it's a good deal, it's important to carefully scrutinize any and all economic development programs. Use realistic assumptions and solid methodologies for cost-benefit analysis. Include accountability measures as well.

It's crucial to put in place a strong system for evaluating incentive deals. A solid cost-benefit analysis is important. Make sure that system is 100 percent transparent.

In fact, it might be wise to use an objective outside group to conduct evaluations. It's important to make sure data is trustworthy. The person making the case to provide the incentive shouldn't be the only one providing information. They may not take all the variables of the community into account.

Make sure that there are clearly defined metrics for determining success. Clearly state the desired results and include clear metrics so the company can later be held accountable. Measures to determine success might be number of jobs created, increase in tax base, amount of money invested in construction materials and labor, cost-benefit analysis, new dollars invested in land, and number of relocated or expanded new businesses.

Here are some criteria to consider when evaluating:

Is the company promising job creation? If so, ask the following questions:

- Are they good jobs? Can employees earn enough to support themselves?

- Are the jobs going to people who live in the community or will employees be driving from two counties over? It's important to keep dollars at home.

- Do the jobs spawn and nurture other businesses?

- How long will the jobs last? Will the company leave in five or ten years when the incentives expire?

What will be the economic ripple effect on other businesses? It's important to consider more than just the impact of the new payroll. There could also be new contractor activity as people build houses. New employees will spend more money in restaurants, stores, car dealerships, etc.

How much demand will this business place on infrastructure and public services? For instance, local shops demand less from city planning departments than nationally known stores entering the community.

What effect will this company have on the local environment? Will it create pollution, sprawl, or traffic congestion?

Will bringing in this company add to or detract from the uniqueness of the community? Entrepreneurs and professionals tend to want to settle down in communities that have character and offer a sense of place.

Here are a few more tips and how-tos:

Don't look at incentivizing only big corporations. They aren't right for every community. Think about what different-size companies might bring to the community. Also don't overlook the businesses that are already in the community.

Don't be afraid to add stipulations before agreeing to an incentive deal. For example, consider asking the company to agree to hire a certain percentage of people who live in the county or even from certain neighborhoods.

Include a performance agreement clause so the deal can be canceled (or the companies penalized) if goals aren't being met.

If an incentive is agreed upon, evaluate the project over time to rate its success and report the results publicly.

Be really transparent about the entire process. (This will help prevent people from calling it a giveaway.) Remember, incentives can be controversial, and people will watch to make sure the company keeps its promises and that the city holds them accountable.

Be consistent in the evaluation process so companies, citizens, and other government officials know exactly what to expect.

There will be less successful results on occasion, but that's just part of the process. We all want to learn from our experiences and make better choices in the future.

Incentives won't be necessary forever. The early trailblazers will probably benefit the most. That's fair because those that come first are taking a much bigger risk. So when certain types of plans are put in place, make sure they are done in such a way that they can be sunset when the community hits certain success milestones.

In the end, the best strategy is to create such a dynamic and business-friendly community that incentives won't be necessary. Companies will want to come there anyway. All in all, it's better to earn their business. It just creates a healthier relationship in the long run.

I like this quote from Amy Liu, vice president and director of metropolitan policy program at Brookings and a national expert on cities and metropolitan areas. She was interviewed by Paul Solman for a PBS *NewsHour* piece on the cities wooing Amazon for its second headquarters. She said:

"The bulk of job creation in a state and city comes not from business attraction deals. They only make up 3 percent of all the jobs created in a community. Real job creation comes from entrepreneurship, start-ups, helping scale new firms, and helping existing companies grow."[1]

In other words, as long as someone is paying attention to the things companies care about—great schools, a willingness to provide leader training and workforce development, solid infrastructure, a livable community, and so forth—incentives won't be such a critical part of your equation. If they work out, fine. If they don't, fine. Other investments will happen because you are doing the right things over time.

Investors are attracted to solid towns. Do the things that matter, that are sustainable, and that make sense for your community. Be a place businesses want to come. Talent and investment will follow. The business community will grow in an organic, sustainable way.

CHAPTER 16

Engagement

Getting people really engaged in community development efforts is important, but it's far from easy. Time is just so tight. People have busy, stressful lives. They may be struggling themselves. They have bills to pay, children to raise, jobs to do, aging parents to care for. It can be hard to take the time to even educate themselves on what the issues are, let alone have time to get involved in the community's projects.

Yet, striving to engage citizens is vitally important. The more successful a community is at doing this, the more likely it is to meet its goals.

When seeking to activate a community, it's important to do all that can be done to engage people as much as possible. They want to be engaged; however, we need to be helpful in making it easier. A successful effort means everyone is involved. Their feedback, their support, and their ideas are all necessary. Making the effort to pursue and implement them is worth it. Once citizens are galvanized, they will turn out, take action, make their voices heard, and applaud leaders for making the community better.

In Pensacola, here are some strategies and tactics that we have found to be successful.

Promote Civic Engagement Around Community Development Projects

It's important to recruit and re-recruit local citizens because they really do have more skin in the game than anyone. People are already engaged in their communities. They already work there, live there, send their children to school there. They just need to get emotionally engaged in the projects that will improve the community.

Here are a few tips:

- Be willing to get in front of key groups and talk to them about why these projects matter and how they can help.

- Ask for their feedback. Use it if possible. This will build trust and get them even more invested and engaged.

- Don't exhaust the community. Give them only one or two actions to take at a time. When I worked in healthcare, I told hospitals to select only one or two items to implement, rather than overwhelming them with a huge list of changes that need to be made. Break them into small, doable steps and sequence them correctly. This makes the process so much more successful. The same is true for communities.

- Keep connecting them back to the *why*. Remember we talked about the burning platform? In our case, we kept reminding the community over and over that the purpose of these projects was to keep their children at home.

Successful neighborhood projects plant the seeds of civic engagement. Together they create a civic engagement infrastructure. People take a lot of pride in what has been accomplished. And once they see the successes, future community initiatives will gain momentum. By then, people are too invested not to care.

Sometimes a big bold event is needed to really draw people's attention to the subject of community engagement. In our case, that event happens every month: CivicCon.

CivicCon: Kicking Off a Civic Conversation

In Pensacola, the Studer Community Institute and the *Pensacola News Journal* partnered to create a speaker's series called CivicCon, which stands for Civic Conversation. The idea is to bring the nation's leading thinkers and experts on community building in to speak on a variety of topics, including creating fiscally sound communities, diversity, infrastructure, education, parking, etc.

We came up with CivicCon because we wanted to hear from the experts, gather best practices, and stay strategic on how we moved forward. In addition, in order to get critical mass around how to improve planning, prosperity, and quality of life, we needed to have a lot of people hearing the same message at the same time. When people hear the same message at the same time, it's amazing how it resonates with them.

In September 2017, we hosted our first event to a packed house of 450 people, with an additional 4,000 people watching it online. This level of engagement was powerful! It exceeded our expectations.

Charles "Chuck" Marohn, founder and president of Strong Towns, was our speaker. He talked about investing in projects that use our current infrastructure instead of shiny new projects that add new infrastructure costs. It's not that there's anything wrong with new projects; it's that there are lots of current roads, pipes, and powerlines with vacant land around them that can more efficiently and cost effectively be used. He showed us how important it is to do infill developments. He talked about the tax advantages of taking downtowns and making them vibrant. And he showed us various examples of communities that took citizen-powered change one block at a time.

This changed the conversation in Pensacola and really got people talking. People started taking a new look at their community. Chuck's speech generated a lot of activity online and in person.

We thought this speech would be a one-and-done for Chuck. But he came back again to talk to a neighborhood within the city of Pensacola called Brownsville, a once-vibrant community that has had some hard times. Once again, we had a full house. He also spoke with Baptist Health Care, which is a hospital system that is very interested in improving the neighborhoods around their community. (Every business should be as concerned about their neighborhood as they are their own business, because they have a symbiotic relationship.) Leaders in

Panama City, FL, heard about the success of CivicCon and brought Chuck in to speak to their community as well.

As this book is being written, there are some exciting CivicCon topics scheduled for 2018. Our six focus areas will be prosperity, infrastructure, smart planning, civic engagement, caring community, and quality of life. Our first three speakers of 2018 will be former Senator Bob Graham, speaking on the importance of civic engagement; three-term Pittsburgh Mayor Tom Murphy, speaking on public-private partnership strategies; and conservationist Edward T. McMahon, speaking on the importance of community character. Other speakers include Emily Talen, professor of urbanism at the University of Chicago, who will talk about cities and social equity, and Gena Wirth, design principal at SCAPE Landscape Architecture, who will speak on urban waterfronts and coastal resilience.

The point is that by bringing in outside experts to talk about what's worked and what hasn't worked in other communities, we expanded the thinking of our own community. We helped educate them. It's almost like we provided all of our citizens an opportunity to get a free degree in urban planning.

Now keep in mind that it's important to bring in experts who don't have a vested interest. We don't want them to be emotionally or financially tied to any specific project. Be very careful not to tell them which projects to support or not support. Just give them free reign to come in and discuss what they see—in terms of walkability, private partnership opportunities, etc.

Keep in mind that none of these projects or events can happen in an information vacuum. People need to be made aware of what's going on. This is why having a good relationship with the media is a must.

Engage the Local Media

The local media plays an important role in what happens in any community. In fact, they are unbelievably vital. Be sure to keep them updated on the progress being made so they can keep residents informed about what is going on. In Pensacola we're in a really good place with our local media.

Remember, over the years the media as an industry has suffered big cutback on ad dollars, and they are understaffed and overworked. Being easy to work with will make all the difference. It will make their jobs a lot easier, and they are much more likely to engage when some basic principles are followed. Here are some simple tips:

Always be transparent. Hopefully, the local media has integrity and is transparent. They expect the same from community leaders. A person once told me, "If you have to lie about something or hide it, it's probably not a good thing to do." To move toward a vibrant community, it's absolutely necessary to be totally open. If they find anything less than full transparency, it's very difficult to win them back. If there's money to be made, let them know about it. They understand that. When Studer Properties closed on a vital piece of property, we invited the media to the closing. We let them see exactly what we were doing. Many people who invest in the community could actually get a better ROI by putting their money in other places. They should be able to get a decent ROI without being villainized. Most are not taking advantage of the situation, but see it as an opportunity to make their community a better place for everyone.

If everything can't be shared, explain why. Sometimes there's confidentiality with a buyer. But most of the time, the truth is going to be found out anyway: whether a property sells, whether it doesn't sell, and so on. There's nothing wrong with sharing and being totally transparent with the data. I've seen plenty of private companies share their data. What's interesting is that people want others to do well financially. It's only when they feel someone is doing well financially on somebody else's back, on somebody else's heartache, that they have a problem.

As long as everything is above board, and the right intentions are behind it, there won't be anything to hide from the media anyway.

Display high integrity and be your own spokesperson. Leaders and decision makers shouldn't put anyone between themselves and the media. Don't put somebody else out front, such as a public relations person (even though they're very vital as a profession). A leader who is driving a project should be the spokesperson.

Be responsive. It's important to be completely open to the media and to be responsive and answer questions. Media people have tight deadlines. They're trying to move something. Give them your cell number. When they call, call back. The sooner the call can be returned the better. If they send a text, text back. Make sure to be available. If they reach out, they are likely working on a story with a deadline and might just be fact-checking information.

Don't slam the media. While it's a popular thing to do, it really doesn't help anything. They do not have an easy job, and their industry has been in constant turmoil. With layoffs and downsizing, there have been lots of stressful changes. With all of these changes, and with media outlets often being understaffed, they face many challenges. Don't add to them. Be patient and understanding.

Don't insult their integrity. People often direct accusations at the media like, "You're giving them good publicity because they spend advertising dollars." That's a great way *not* to have a good relationship: to accuse somebody of lacking integrity. Besides, it's not true. My company and I have spent the same amount of advertising dollars for the past decade. There were times, four or five years ago, when, if I had made this decision based on positive coverage, I wouldn't have spent a dime. If you advertise, don't pull dollars when you're not happy. It's short-sighted.

Engage on Social Media

Social media is also critical. Don't be afraid to be very engaged and active on social media. This is a big part of branding your community. For a company, social media enhances the customer experience because customers get to communicate with them directly. There's no filter. For a community, *citizens* are the customers.

Social media allows citizens to be heard, to share their likes, dislikes, and ideas, and to connect with leaders in a real, authentic way. It's extremely important to be educated on social media and on branding in general. It's an important part of building up a vibrant community.

So be available, be responsive, be transparent, and make sure that people see the information. And of course, don't be combative. Following these guidelines will help to create a great relationship with the media. The media are vital to carrying a message, because people watch them and count on them to know what's going on.

Reward and Recognize Volunteers

At this point, a lot of people will have given a lot of time to make things happen. Be sure to thank them and reward and recognize them in meaningful ways. This is more than a nice thing to do; it's a practical and very powerful tool for reinforcing specific behaviors. Recognized behavior gets repeated. This is the heart of engagement.

In my work in healthcare and other business arenas, I encouraged people to regularly send thank-you notes and use other methods of reward and recognition. People really appreciate it. Pretty soon the whole company is full of people making it a point to replicate the behavior that got them recognized. The impact of that can be enormous. I find this to be just as true on a community-wide basis as it is inside organizations.

In Pensacola we try to publicly tell the story of what our volunteers are doing. We write things in the paper thanking them for being difference makers. What volunteers want the most is not only to be thanked but to feel connected to the difference they are making.

Getting people engaged in revitalizing the community is a huge task. It is an ongoing task. It is a never-ending task. But it is also a labor of love. The subtitle of this book refers to citizen-powered change. That's because the people who work, play, raise children, create schools, and run businesses are the lifeblood of any community. The citizens *are* the community. And only by giving their time, energy, and talents can any community change and grow in a positive direction as we move into the future.

CHAPTER 17

The Titans of Revitalization

A Blueprint for Galvanizing and Growing Your Small Business Community

Section One:
Necessary Conditions for a Small Business Revolution

Section Two:
The Pensacola Way: Helping Small Businesspeople Thrive Through Training and Development

Section Three:
Creating a Training Program: The Must-Have Skills for Entrepreneurs

Section Four:
Mentors Matter: How to Be One…and How to Work With One

Section Five:
How to Create Your Own Small Business Challenge

SECTION 1

Necessary Conditions for a Small Business Revolution

No doubt about it: Small businesses are leading the way to revitalize America. According to the U.S. Small Business Administration's August 2017 *Small Business Quarterly Bulletin*, they've created two out of every three net new jobs since 2014. They key to creating a vibrant community is engaging and empowering small business owners.

Fostering a strong sense of community in this population and harnessing their energy and know-how creates a powerful army of citizens who can be galvanized to help solve many of the problems communities are facing. They will be catalysts for change and sustainers. They will take charge of making sure good, sustainable growth stays on track. They'll make sure young people are getting educated, downtown is thriving, and government is running smoothly. They have an active interest in keeping their community strong. Their livelihood often depends on it.

Most communities want small businesses to thrive. They realize that a healthy small business presence equals a healthy community and vice versa. They just don't always know how to create the right conditions. Here are just of few of the things we learned along the way.

First, it's a matter of realizing that small business success doesn't "just happen." The conditions need to be right, and communities need to be proactive and deliberate about creating those conditions.

Communities need to create the kind of environment that 1) ignites the spirit of entrepreneurship and 2) keeps small businesses alive and supported by everyone in the community.

After being involved in Pensacola's journey, observing other cities and towns over the years, and listening to insights and advice graciously shared by many community leaders, I've realized there are ten essential factors small businesses need to thrive.

Ten Must-Haves for Sparking and Sustaining a Small Business Revolution

1. **A friendly regulatory environment.** Small businesses need easy-to-understand codes from local government as well as a solid understanding of *why* such regulations are in place. Too often (accurately or not) entrepreneurs and small business owners perceive that local governments put up hurdles for them to jump over.

2. **A strong entrepreneurial support system.** When we started our small business roundtables in Pensacola, the most noted feedback we got is that entrepreneurs often feel isolated. Small business owners need support and collegiality. Communities need to start and promote clubs and groups that allow them to connect with other entrepreneurs.

3. **A culture of community support.** Entrepreneurs need to feel that the community is invested in their well-being. Once leaders start this conversation, the community will respond.

    The feeling Pensacola citizens have toward small businesses can be described only as pure connectedness. Once we made the case that small businesses make communities better, our citizens became huge supporters. People jumped right in. They'll do anything to help make a small business successful.

4. **Access to good employees/talent pool.** A successful community has to be a place where people want to live. Safe neighborhoods, a strong education system, a vibrant downtown, and other amenities that add up to a good quality of life are must-haves.

    This is one reason Pensacola is focused on creating America's first Early Learning City and boosting kindergarten readiness. Research shows that jobs and education are the two areas key to quality of life.

5. **Strong mentors in the community to help entrepreneurs navigate what they don't know.** Not only does this keep them from making costly mistakes, it helps them feel supported so they don't mind taking the risks necessary for growth.

It's impressive to see how many busy, seasoned business owners have stepped into a mentorship role in Pensacola. It has created lasting relationships and has been very fulfilling for both parties.

6. **Orchestrated growth around them.** Growth begets more growth. When companies, non-profits, and other organizations are thriving, new ventures are more likely to take off and thrive themselves. That growth needs to be strategic and thoughtful. For a small business owner, what's to the left, right, and across the street from the storefront really matters. That's why in Pensacola we've kept a careful eye on where businesses are placed.

7. **A safe, clean environment in which to operate.** Attractive urban and suburban spaces and low crime rates are good for business. Customers won't come to businesses in an unsafe area, no matter how good the product or service is.

8. **Access to capital.** Bank loans, government grants, and other forms of assistance can go a long way toward helping small businesses invest in their future. And sometimes mentors can help connect them to silent partners for funding.

9. **Access to workforce development training.** Entrepreneurs often have expertise around products or services, but little working knowledge about how to actually run a business. This is why it's so important that entrepreneurs learn the basics of leadership and sound business practices. If they don't, they will likely fail, even if their product or service is superior.

10. **A commitment to promoting innovation and start-ups.** Local governments have a tendency to court big business and big industry, usually at the expense of new ventures and mom & pops. This trend needs to shift. Cities need to invest in their small shops, restaurants, and small and mid-size businesses and make decisions that benefit them just as much as (if not more than) the big box retailers and manufacturing giants.

    BONUS: Consider hosting a small business challenge. This is a contest in which people compete to submit the best small business idea. The winner gets funding and support for getting their new venture started. This really gives a big boost to start-ups and small companies. It forces them to organize and put their plans on paper. It drives them forward.

When Studer Properties issued its own challenge for Pensacola, we got amazing results. Not only did we help promote one very successful small business owner, other companies got started as a result. There were also people who, after doing all the leg work, realized that they just weren't ready. That's important, too. (See "Here Are Ten Skills Every Entrepreneur and Small Business Owner Must Have" for more info.)

Small businesses truly are the lifeblood of America. They've built our nation, employed our people, fueled our national work ethic, and given our children a dream to work toward. As community leaders and as ordinary citizens, we owe it to them to support, encourage, and foster their well-being and growth.

Communities can strive to create good environments for small business. We in Pensacola have learned from others—and we are still learning—and we hope we can help others as we have been helped. We find that all towns and cities want the same thing: to become a great place for people to live and visit. We are all on the same journey to make people's lives better.

SECTION 2

The Pensacola Way: Helping Small Businesspeople Thrive Through Training and Development

In Pensacola, we knew that a thriving community would depend on our ability to create and grow thriving businesses. Successful owners create jobs. They pay rent and taxes. They also give back to the community in so many other ways. We decided to focus not only on helping start-ups get off the ground, but to help them continue to grow and thrive. We knew that well-trained business owners make better decisions and fewer mistakes. That's why we centered our strategy on providing the workforce development they need.

Studer Community Institute (SCI), a nonprofit organization focused on improving Pensacola's quality of life, started out by offering small, focused training sessions around a few topics. Our efforts have now evolved into a comprehensive training program that engages much of our business community. SCI offers leadership development training through a series of workshops, roundtables, and a yearly conference all aimed at entrepreneurs and small business owners.

Our approach includes a focus on these three areas: monthly workshops, business roundtables, and a yearly conference. Here's an overview of each:

Monthly Training and Development Workshops

We began our workshop series by identifying the leadership skills it takes to run a successful business: for example, hiring, firing, employee engagement, creating revenue streams, process improvement, marketing, etc.

We know business owners are busy and that everyone may not need training on every skill, so we created a tool that evaluates which of them a business owner most needs to be trained in. For example, if a business has only three employees, hiring is probably not the most important thing in the world to them, but creating revenue streams might be really important.

To do this foundational training, we've been able to pull a lot of experts from the community— many of whom are business owners—to teach specific skills. These monthly workshops have been an amazing success, and people are stunned at the talent we have here.

Small Business Roundtables

Another component of workforce development is the small business "round-tables," where owners get together with a facilitator and talk about the issues they're facing. These business roundtables meet every 90 days. They are done in small groups—generally four to eight small business owners—so that participants can be comfortable sharing their problems and ideas. We choose a good facilitator who can answer questions and keep the discussion productive and on track.

Like the workshops, the purpose of the roundtables is training and leadership development. However, they're more intense and focused. At each session, we focus on providing tools people can implement immediately to solve some of their biggest problems. Over time, this training becomes a very powerful skill set.

We get great feedback from these sessions. One of the things we hear most often is that business owners often feel alone and think they are the only one having problems. The roundtables show them this is not true. And while the training and development are important, one of the most meaningful byproducts is that participants all end up helping each other.

Once people get to know each other, they start to share resources and create strong relationships. Before long they're all working together and thinking in a different way: *How can I do this for you? How can you do this for me? How can we form a partnership? Can we start a new business?*

EntreCon

EntreCon is an annual business conference held in Pensacola each November. It provides a venue for local entrepreneurs, professionals, and leaders to come together, learn from experts on most pressing problems, and learn from each other. The idea is to continue to share the tactical tools and strategies attendees need to hone their leadership, grow their business, and improve their bottom line.

We bring in nationally known experts from the business community to share their expertise in areas businesspeople often struggle with, and we offer breakouts featuring local talent. By hosting EntreCon locally, we're providing a cost-effective, convenient way for local companies to get world-class training without the expense of travel.

Every year, this conference grows and generates more energy and excitement than the previous year. Clearly, it is meeting a need and resonating with a lot of businesspeople.

The Power of an Engaged Business Community

Pensacola's workshops, roundtables, and conference are successful separately, but together they help make learning a habit for busy entrepreneurs. Once people start learning, they want to keep learning. They make the monthly training a priority and they start actively seeking more opportunities. Those who participate in monthly training usually participate in roundtables and attend EntreCon. It all works together to create a powerful business community that is truly engaged.

The ROI on training is truly amazing. Well-trained business owners not only run healthier businesses that are more sustainable, but once they get engaged, they are more than willing to share their best practices, offer support, make connections, brainstorm new ideas, and give back. Specifically, the business leaders who lead workshops, facilitate roundtables, and hold learning sessions at EntreCon often become mentors to new entrepreneurs. Then, as business owners get over the hump, they come back and help others.

Kristine Rushing is a great example of how this can work. She was a highly energetic young businesswoman who had an insurance agency. She wanted to improve her business skills and started attending some of the workforce development sessions being offered. She ended up coming back and training others on hiring talent and creating the right culture in your company. She got so good at it that eventually the company she owned with her husband, Reid, merged with Beck Property Company (to form Beck Partners), as they were really interested in workplace culture and she had become a recognized expert.

All of these training programs not only help participants grow their own companies, they generate a synergy that creates something bigger. This is a great example of the "circle" principle in action. When people in one circle are introduced to people in another circle, pretty soon the edges start to blend and merge into a bigger, more powerful, more unified group. And when a community is able to connect people who would not normally meet, amazing things can happen.

Putting these folks together on a regular basis has helped gel our business community, and they love learning from each other. People start to see competitors as collaborators. They begin to trust each other. They form partnerships. They end up talking about the problems they face as a community—such as economic opportunity, education, the talent drain—and they begin to brainstorm solutions and work together in other ways.

By getting people together and helping them form meaningful connections, we're galvanizing an army of citizens who just happen to be small business owners. Our small business sector is becoming a well-orchestrated community, and there is so much power in community. There is a lot of positive energy generated around the mission of creating a stronger and better Pensacola.

SECTION 3

Creating a Training Program: The Must-Have Skills for Entrepreneurs

Starting a business isn't easy, and keeping it going is even harder. It is estimated that 40 percent of new businesses fail in their first year and that 80 percent don't make it five years.[1]

In *The E-Myth Revisited*, Michael Gerber explains why. He says most companies are started by "technicians." A plumber decides to start a plumbing company, or a person who loves to cook decides to open her own restaurant. These people are passionate about what they do and they have expertise around their service or product. What they don't have are the skills to run a company. For example, they don't know how to manage people and processes or handle the money side. So they fail.

When building out the training program for your entrepreneurial community, focus on foundational skills that will help business owners be successful.

Here Are Ten Skills Every Entrepreneur and Small Business Owner Must Have:

1. **A grasp of financial management.** One doesn't have to be a financial wizard, but a basic understanding of how to manage finances is a must. In particular, a good handle on cash flow and receivables is important.

2. **Solid marketing expertise.** People tend to use this word as a synonym for advertising, but it's way bigger than that. Marketing is *all* the decisions that take place in the process of getting your product to the consumer. All small business owners need to be heavily involved in effective marketing. Generally speaking, *pull* marketing, in which you motivate customers to seek out your brand and work to create a loyal following is more effective than *push* marketing in which you attempt to take your product directly to them and convince them to buy.

3. **The ability to sell.** Sometimes people have great ideas but are not great at compelling others to act on them. While it is a plus, it's not necessary to be a super-talkative extrovert. It is far more important to be passionate about the product and willing to talk about why. A good leader will also be a powerful force on the sales team. Employees will look to leadership to learn how to articulate the benefits of your product.

4. **A bias toward execution.** Strategy and innovation matter, but successful businesspeople know when to pull the trigger and get things done already. There are lots of great ideas floating around, but if they can't be put into motion, they're useless.

5. **An instinct for customer experience.** Now that Amazon and other online retailers have changed the game forever, success is more about service than it's ever been. Smart entrepreneurs know: Take care of customers, and they'll take care of you.

6. **The leadership know-how to create an engaging culture.** The only way to compete with large companies is with a well-run organization that people want to work for. Attracting and keeping great talent means deliberately creating a culture where people are engaged, energized, and excited about their ability to make a difference. (And in a small company, a single person *can* make a huge impact: That's one edge a small business can have over big corporations.)

7. **Smart delegation and careful time management.** These are two issues that entrepreneurs definitely struggle with. They want to be involved in everything and are usually driven to work 24/7. However, a successful entrepreneur works *on* their business, not *in* their business—and this can be done only through smart delegation and careful time management.

8. **Problem-solving savvy.** Every start-up or new business has problems that pop up as it's finding its wings. Some are small, some are bigger, and some are life-threatening. Smart leaders know: a) how to catch problems early before they get out of control, and b) whom to turn to for help finding a solution.

9. **The right balance of "network" and "hard work."** A lot of small businesspeople love the "grip and grin" part of networking. They like meeting people and brainstorming with them but somehow don't get around to

the deep thinking and elbow grease part of the equation. Networking is great, and to some degree necessary, but make sure to cultivate a reputation for being a hard worker and big producer.

10. **Civic-mindedness.** The most successful entrepreneurs are those who don't focus on winning and taking all the time. They're the ones who want to help, share, mentor other small business owners, and in general make the world a better place. Reciprocity seems to be a law of the Universe: Give back to the community, and the community will take care of you.

SECTION 4

Mentors Matter: How to Be One...and How to Work With One

Mentoring can be an extremely powerful part of workforce development and building a vibrant community. The strongest and best communities are those where entrepreneurs and small businesses are supported and allowed to flourish. No one starts out knowing how to run a strong business. That's why it's so important for communities to find a way to share guidance with aspiring entrepreneurs and help small businesses get started and grow.

In fact, in his book *The Coming Jobs War*, Gallup Chairman and CEO Jim Clifton describes the need for what he calls "super mentors."

"The heroes America needs for this moment in history will come from those who guide, advise, encourage, and mentor small businesses to success," Clifton writes, "which is the conception moment that saves a city and a country."

Clifton continues, "Super mentors can be almost anyone, but they are not the innovators nor the entrepreneurs. They are the ones who light fires under the innovators and entrepreneurs. Super mentors are willing to take a risk for an individual and an idea. They are the tipping point of extra energy that causes the action to occur. They also encourage existing small and medium-sized companies to take risks. They do things like help entrepreneurs get a banker or a good lead, give advice, lend a hand or a shoulder at critical moments, and often join their board. That's an essential aspect of originating new jobs.

"Super mentors create the almighty behavioral economic variables of confidence and action."[2]

Mentoring relationships often happen naturally, but it's critical to get very intentional about creating structured mentoring programs in business communities. Otherwise, too much is left to chance. In order for mentoring to be successful, it's really important to understand that it's a partnership between individuals—a mentor and a mentee—to promote professional and career development. This means that both parties need to engage and there should be a real focus on outcomes.

Whether you're thinking of being a mentor to someone in your community, or looking for a mentor for yourself, it can help to know what great mentors look like. Here are just a few qualities of a great mentor.

Great mentors have done it and/or are doing it. They are respected in their organizations and in the community.

Great mentors are willing to share their knowledge, expertise, and skills... They understand where the mentee is, they relate to the time when they were there themselves, they show sincerity, and they freely give away what they have learned.

...But they don't just give the answers. Instead, they help the mentee arrive at the answers. Great mentors want mentees to think for themselves. They listen fully and ask probing questions. Sometimes they ask mentees to go away and think about an issue for a while and report back.

They focus on character at least as much as skill. They know that values, self-awareness, integrity, and empathy matter more than knowing how to perform tasks. A mentee can always learn how to *do* something. Guidance on how to *be* will serve them better in the long run.

Great mentors aren't afraid to get personal. They know there is no sharp divide between work life and personal life. It's a real relationship. Sometimes the lines get blurred and that's okay.

Great mentors walk the walk. They demonstrate the same behaviors they are teaching.

They are honest about their shortcomings. If a mentor isn't yet where they want to be in their career and life, they say so. Mentors are human and not perfect. It is not fair to a mentor or a mentee for the mentor to be put on a pedestal.

Great mentors care. They take the role of a mentor seriously. They're like a guide on a mountain climb: They want to make sure the tools and skills are in place. They are committed to the mentee's success.

They are positive by nature. Mentors are cup half-full people who help the mentee see the opportunities when facing obstacles. The mentee can feel the enthusiasm of the mentor, both spoken and unspoken.

Great mentors know they are not finished products. They have committed themselves to ongoing learning. They admit when they are still learning in the mentor-mentee relationship. They will often learn right along with the mentee.

They help the mentee hold up the mirror. They provide constructive feedback and guidance. Mentors help the mentee leverage their strengths. A mentor will also benefit from the lessons as it will help them hold up their own mirror.

Great mentors teach from experience. They do not ask a mentee to take steps they themselves did not take. They share their own self-awareness and development plan and their own goals.

They demand accountability. If the mentee isn't living up to their end of the bargain or if they otherwise aren't doing their best, a great mentor is willing to say so.

They also help the mentee find other mentors. Even the best mentor will also have gaps in their knowledge. They don't mind admitting this. Due to their experience and network, they can usually connect the mentee with other resources. In addition, they should know how much they can help and when it's time to get someone else involved.

Great mentors tell the hard truths (but they do it with caring). They explain that even when feedback is not positive, it is because they care and are committed to the mentee's success. They connect to the *why*. And when tempers flare, which sometimes happens, they are patient with the mentee.

These are really just tips I've collected over the years. I know there are many more out there. If you're thinking of becoming a mentor, consider doing some research. There are great resources out there for setting up a very effective program.

Maximizing the Mentoring Experience

Now, let's talk briefly about the other party in this relationship: the mentee. Anyone, no matter how experienced they are, can benefit from being a mentee—particularly if they are entering a new field or taking on an ownership role for the first time.

If you are a mentee looking for a mentor, do some research. Then, list three to five people who may fit what can help you most. After that, just ask. You'll be surprised at how many would say yes.

Some may decline when asked and that's okay. Don't take it personally. There could be good reasons for some to say no, like family, health, etc. Many will be surprised you asked them because they may be selling themselves short on the impact they are making and the impact they could have on a mentee.

The ideal mentee is a motivated individual who is open to feedback, coaching, and guidance. They also need the ability to learn, as well as patience and comfort with being a team player.

Here are a few tips for being a good mentee:

Clearly communicate needs. As one might assume, ambiguity can make a mentor/mentee much less effective. It's important for a mentee to communicate the most pressing needs clearly and timely so the mentor can help.

Share thoughts, worries, fears, and hopes for the future. That's what a mentor is for. A good mentee is honest about where they are and where they stand. Even the best mentor can't really help if they don't know the truth. Offer both short- and long-range plans.

Get familiar with the mentor's background. What strengths do they bring to the table? A mentor can have decades of experience that can be vitally important to a newcomer's success. Perhaps their strength isn't to be able to provide financial backing. Understanding the background and skillset a mentor has will help maximize the guidance they can provide.

Take ownership of the relationship. It's important for the mentee to own the communication. Setting up meetings and phone calls keeps the relationship alive.

Be prepared. One effective way would be to prepare a meeting agenda in advance to keep the conversation productive and on task.

Ask for feedback. Don't wait for the mentor to provide it. For example: "What questions should I be asking that I have not asked?" and "On a scale from 1 to 10, with 10 being highest, rate my follow-up actions since we last met."

Be self-aware. Identify specific areas in which you know you need improvement and work on them. A mentor is there to develop, but it can affect the relationship negatively if the mentor finds him or herself working harder at the mentee's success than the mentee is. Identify and execute.

One of my favorite sayings is, "When the student is ready, the teacher appears." A good mentee stays ready and looking for the right mentor to appear, so that when the right person comes along, they are able to fully capitalize on it.

SECTION 5

How to Create Your Own Small Business Challenge

A great way to jump-start interest in growing a small business community is to issue a small business challenge. This was a big win for Pensacola.

Creating a small business challenge was one of our first steps in getting a laser focus on small business. We wanted to inspire a passion for small business and we wanted to give people a compelling reason to turn their great ideas into viable business plans. This kind of challenge works because it forces people to put their ideas on paper and creates a sense of urgency around starting a business.

We issued our challenge at the end of 2011 (after having been inspired by Asheville, NC, which did something similar). Essentially, anyone wanting to start or expand a business in downtown Pensacola was invited to submit business plans to a nine-person panel of local business experts. Consultants from the Florida Small Business Development Center at the University of West Florida College of Business (Florida SBDC at UWF) helped the contestants with this process.

For the prize package, we decided on a mix of start-up capital, free and reduced rent, and ongoing mentoring from local business experts. More than 100 participants signed up and paid the $40 business plan software fee. Of that number, 31 made it through the two-month business plan process.

MariCarmen Josephs, an area restaurant manager and chef, was announced the winner in March of 2012. Her proposed restaurant would offer an eclectic blend of Southern and international flavors, including Spanish, Italian, Mexican, Indian, Thai, and Moroccan. Today it's very successful. Carmen's Lunch Bar is a hot meeting place for business lunches, dinners, and pre-event wine and tapas.

We expected this to be a small win, but it has had a huge impact. Not only did Carmen's Lunch Bar quickly get up and running, but several entrepreneurs who went through the process ended up starting companies too: a tamale restaurant, a bakery, a jewelry store, a paddleboard rental company, and a Segway tour company.

There were also some other positive unintended consequences of the challenge. The local newspaper, the *Pensacola News Journal,* was wonderful. They gave us publicity along the way. We also had marketing companies, law firms, and others offer to do free work for the winner, including helping them advertise, write their legal documents, and more. It helped build their businesses.

The challenge also showed us that our business community had a big need for training and support and was the foundation of the Studer Community Institute (SCI) training and development programs we created. It also showcased the value of mentoring. MariCarmen Josephs, our winner, explained that the prize money was needed and appreciated. However, she emphasized that the guidance and support really made a huge difference.

Here are a few tips that we found useful in putting on this challenge.

The How

Put together a team of local business experts to serve as judges.

Figure out the selection criteria. The keys to our selection were a) *Did the business fit with the revitalization needed downtown?* and b) *What were the chances that the business plan plus the skills of the founder would create a sustainable business?*

Decide what the prize package is going to be. In Pensacola's case, we decided that the winner would receive a three-year lease of about 800 square feet in an optimally located building at Palafox and Main, the main intersection in downtown Pensacola. She would receive the first year's rent for free and reduced rent for the next two years. In addition, she would receive a start-up fund of $25,000 for furniture, equipment, and other needed expenses. (The total value of the prize was valued at $50,000.)

Get coaches and mentors in place. Think about who would be most helpful to a new entrepreneur (e.g., marketing people, tax and finance people, attorneys). Offer help with crafting business plans. If there is a local college, get them involved. This team may advise contestants during the challenge and later help the winner kick off his/her venture.

In Pensacola, there was coaching and mentoring throughout the process. In fact, all participants were provided one-on-one mentoring from SBDC staff. They also had access to training and development sessions on creating business plans; specific topics were financial projections, marketing, and marketing analysis.

Set a date for business plans to be turned in. Build in enough time for people to put together a good business plan but not so much time that you lose urgency.

Market the business challenge. Set up a website and/or Facebook page. Enlist local media.

Once a winner is chosen, make sure he or she has plenty of ongoing support. Consider making meetings with support people mandatory.

After MariCarmen Josephs won the Pensacola Business Challenge, she received ongoing mentoring and business training for the first three years of the business.

Specifically, she worked closely with Andrew Rothfeder, president of Studer Properties, from the time she won until about six months after her restaurant opened. He provided guidance in construction, financing, and marketing.

Also she was given access to accounting, marketing/PR, and legal resources—namely, Warren Averett CPAs & Advisors, Impact Campaigns, and Clark Partington Attorneys at Law—to get her through the initial learning curve. (As she became more and more confident, her need for this support tapered off.)

Creating a business challenge should be thought of as a long-term project. Keep the support and the education going, not just for the winner but for the entire business community.

Here are just a few of the benefits a business challenge can bring.

The Benefits

It's not just about the one winner and his or her successful business (in our case, Carmen's Lunch Bar). That's just the beginning. We found the unintended benefits to be incredible.

Forcing others through the process is likely to spawn other small businesses. The ones who don't win will probably still end up opening their own companies. The process forces them to crystallize their ideas and gives them the right foundation.

The challenge then starts to galvanize those small businesspeople. They get to know each other. They get the kind of coaching and mentoring they need to be successful. Also, the process helps identify who's *not* ready to start a small business. This makes failed ventures less likely, which is just as important.

The relationship between a vibrant community and small business is very symbiotic—one can't thrive without the other. Once your small business community gets involved in the process, big things will start to happen in a really organic way. Private enterprise leading the way will create a community that will adapt and adjust to changing circumstances and sustain itself over time.

CHAPTER 18

Changing the Conversation

Being part of any change is hard. Family changes, job changes, and personal changes all come with difficulty. Even positive change can be stressful: a new baby, a new job, a new house or apartment. More and more, we read that stress can be positive or negative. It can motivate and energize us, or it can make us feel anxious and overwhelmed. Certainly, the key is how we react to each change.

Change in a community can be some of the hardest. At times it feels like a no-win situation. If one does not point out the negatives, they are seen as sugarcoaters and ignoring the facts. If one points out facts that are not positive, then they are seen as negative people or downers. Balancing these two extremes is like being asked to drive a nitroglycerin truck with minimal training and without a map.

Being part of the revitalization of a community over the past 14 years has been the best of times and the worst of times. I have seen the best in some people and the worst in others. In holding up my own mirror, I have at times seen the best in me, and other times I have been disappointed in myself. I know anger and resentment are not healthy; however, I admit these two feelings have been there (though hopefully not for long). My journey to recovery from alcoholism over the past 35 years has provided steps that have been critical to successfully managing this revitalization process. Like the journey to recovery, being a part of changing the culture inside a community takes time, acceptance, help from others, and the willingness to be both a student and a teacher. And that journey often starts with changing the conversation.

The first step is deflation of the ego. In traveling to hundreds of communities over the years, I have never been in one where leaders do not feel proud of where they live. Who wants to spend their life in a place they don't like? It is good to notice the positives, and, in fact, this needs to be part of making a community better. Yet, it's the easy part. The hard part is deflating the ego. It requires humility to see the community as it is. This ability—which at times is a gift—to see the community objectively is necessary for diagnosing and then creating a plan to improve what needs to be made better.

Yes, it's great that the Pensacola area has a rich history and beautiful beaches and is the home of the Blue Angels flight team. However, to change we had to come to grips with the fact that too many children are not ready for kindergarten and that there is too much poverty. There was a dying downtown and a flat tax base. Until a community can see themselves clearly and learn to see problems as opportunities, little progress will be made. When reviewing the 17-metric dashboard, it became apparent that time is better spent changing behavior than fighting the data.

Another step in changing the conversation is getting people engaged in solutions. People want to be engaged. It is easy to look at the low percentage of people who take time to vote and to assume they are not interested. That is a mistake. Too often they have been let down and have not been given the reason why, nor have they embraced the belief that they can make a difference. In any change situation, leaders must take time to identify the "burning platform" that will capture people's hearts and minds, creating a sense of urgency.

When the idea of CivicCon was conceived as a way to bring in key community building experts, it was exciting. Yet a concern was that we would bring in these national experts and few people would come. How wrong we were. The Pensacola Little Theatre, where Chuck Marohn from Strong Towns spoke, was packed to its 450-person capacity, and an additional 4,000 people watched the presentation on video. These were the same people who were "completely booked," with "so much to do." However, they showed up. Why? I believe it is due to the fact that they were being listened to, combined with some frustration from not being listened to enough in the past, and a deep-down desire to make a difference.

Don't assume people don't want to be engaged. They do. However, a community needs to work hard at making it relevant and easy.

A third step is realizing that bigger and newer is not always better. The big new project gets the attention, but in the long run it may not be the right project. Our conversation now has to center around how to develop and sustain communities that serve all of us and satisfy our human desire to be connected, all without putting unfair liabilities on future generations. Capitalize on what you already have. This does not mean new and bigger is bad. It does mean there are many options to create a better community.

Community pride has a huge multiplier effect. Once success starts happening, it is so much easier to get people engaged. Once people see positive things happen, they become even prouder of their community. They keep the ball rolling. People will contribute to greater and greater achievements. Optimism, hope, and purpose are the greatest motivators in the world. With them, miracles can happen.

No doubt about it, our cities are in trouble. Not only are they saddled with insurmountable debt, but some are on their way to becoming functionally insolvent. Many cities are not that different from Detroit. Detroit is just 20 years ahead of us because they got started earlier on this style of development (abandoned downtown, no sense of place or smart growth, freeway expansion, etc.) that is bankrupting us. In addition, cities are ill-equipped to develop and design the kind of neighborhoods that make sense for the way people want to live. Our current development models have not served us well, and we know that. We must move forward in a different way. We are asking future generations to subsidize the decisions we are making now, so we owe it to our kids and our grandchildren to make some real changes.

As I mentioned, for our very first CivicCon, we were lucky enough to have Chuck Marohn, founder and president of Strong Towns, speak about this very topic. He did a great job of laying out why the current development model isn't working and what we must do to save our neighborhoods. Here are just a few of the insights from that presentation.

The system is broken. We can no longer support the infrastructure costs of big suburban development, and incentives for large industrial complexes just don't work. We can't keep taking a loss on residential, hoping to make it back on industrial and commercial property. It just doesn't happen.

Engage in smart growth. We must know where revenue comes from. We have to stop confusing activity with progress. Growth gives the illusion of wealth, but not all growth is healthy for a city. We must take a long, hard look at where our revenue comes from and, more importantly, what *isn't* generating revenue. There are a lot of misconceptions in this area. For example, a big box store on the edge of town might seem attractive. However, once we give tax incentives, build a new bypass, and run water and sewer, the net revenue isn't very much. Plus, if they leave, it's a very difficult space to fill. We have to stop chasing big projects and have an honest assessment as to where our revenue is coming from.

Focus on flexible development. We need development that is productive, adaptable, and flexible. Downtown buildings are a great example of this. If more residential is needed—or more office or more retail—it's easy to shift in whatever direction is necessary. If one store goes out of business, it doesn't decimate the whole community.

New is not always better. We must look for solutions without always thinking new is better. We often have underutilized or non-performing assets that could be converted. Of course there are times when new construction is a better solution, but evaluating existing options should be step one. Don't overlook the smaller projects that generate revenue. We must fill in vacant land and thicken our streets.

Start now, even if your neighborhood is doing well. Get intentional. Don't waste time looking back to what you should have done or finger-pointing. Remember the Chinese proverb, "The best time to plant a tree is 20 years ago; the second best time is today." This has resonated with me since this journey started.

The good news is that people are capable of achieving great things. Bill Gates wrote a blog post I really like titled "How Did Humans Get Smart?" In it he writes about a book he likes titled *Sapiens: A Brief History of Humankind* by Yuval Noah Harari. Gates writes:

"Other species had big brains too, but what made *Homo sapiens* so successful is that we are the only animals who are capable of large-scale cooperation. We know how to organize ourselves as nations, companies, and religions, giving us the power to accomplish complex tasks."[1]

It is this large-scale cooperation that will help us revitalize our communities and, ultimately, our nation. America has long celebrated the rugged individual. Certainly there is a place for him or her. But now is the time for us to come back together as a community.

As you make your community better, you will have the gratification of seeing lives get better. Some people will thank you. Many others will never know the part you played. You are not doing it for recognition. Great things take place when no one cares who gets the credit. The best part is people will have a better quality of life. That's what this journey was about from the start, and it's what it continues to be for you and countless others.

When our group presented the park project to the city council, we used this Nelson Mandela quote to frame our project: "It always seems impossible, until it is done." At the time I don't think any of us knew what was ahead of us and what the road would be. And yet so much has been accomplished. We still have a lot of work to do, but our community is moving along nicely, with a sense of passion and cooperation that comes when you start to see what is possible. Pensacola is proof that, as Aristotle said, "The whole is greater than the sum of its parts." When individuals come together with a common goal, it creates a synergy that is unstoppable.

Thank you for having such great purpose, doing worthwhile work, and making a difference. Never underestimate the difference you can make.

Acknowledgments

This book is a book about love: a love for a community, which is really a love for people. Just like you love those in your community.

There were two events in the early 1980s that set the foundation for the journey I have been and continue to be on. The first took place on December 25, 1982. I had what is described as a moment of clarity. I was able to view myself in a completely objective manner. What appeared was not pretty. I saw a twice-divorced father of two who was using alcohol way too much. I recently passed 35 years of sobriety. Yet looking back on this wake-up call, I now see that it was step one of becoming a more useful person. It also helped me understand how vital to growth it is to be able to hold up one's own mirror. The same is true of a community.

The second event was February 24, 1984, when I married my current wife, Rishy. It takes a special person to marry someone in recovery and be on the journey with them. Likely, these are the same type of people who enjoy roller coaster rides. So often this journey would have stopped if Rishy had felt any reservations. It's a big risk to quit a well-paying hospital presidency job to start a company. Yet that's what I did. To be married to someone who goes from a great salary, super benefits, and good security to venturing into an uncharted future is not for the faint-hearted. Then to be patient while that spouse works in a new company as it grows, and to have a husband on the road for most of 12 years with young children at home is not easy. It takes a special person to say yes to buying an independent baseball team and then to tirelessly work in the organization doing everything from setting up chairs, to making shirts, to handling the team laundry. Finally, Rishy was there as we embarked on the emotional trip that was the Community Maritime Park and the referendum, from rehabbing buildings and starting and working in all the retail stores, to selecting bricks and furniture for the new projects, to a hundred items in between. I have done little to receive this unconditional love; however, I am grateful for it.

There's no way to express the deep thoughts I have on my sister, Susan, and my father, Quin, whom we lost in 2014 and 2015, respectively. They were such great supporters and they are missed. Thank you to my mother, Shirley, who has always been a fan. I'm grateful for inheriting a bit of her thick skin, which has proven helpful on this journey. Thanks also to my mother's great friends Laverne and Dick Baker and Ruth and Frank Miller. You mean so much to her.

This book would not have happened without Dottie DeHart of DeHart & Company Public Relations. Her encouragement to tell the story, and to research and help organize the material in this book, has been invaluable. Thanks also to Barbara Scott Payne for keeping the book on track and managing the details.

Usually people know *what* they would like to see happen; the great challenge is *how*. In this case, how could we improve the quality of life for ourselves and others in Pensacola? We learned how from so many: Jim Clifton, Ray Gindroz, Bruce Barcelo, and Mike Thiessen—all outside experts who served as teachers at various times in this journey. We also learned a lot from the cities that shared what their own journey has been like.

A big thanks goes to Tom Bonfield, city manager of Pensacola from 1998-2008. Without him, it's possible that none of this would have taken place. His phone call to me changed me and hopefully changed the community for the better. He did lots of heavy lifting until he left the city in 2008. Thank you also to Dick Barker, CFO for the city of Pensacola, who was vital in figuring out the funding for the Vince J. Whibbs Sr. Community Maritime Park.

I would also like to thank the three mayors who were involved in this project from start to finish: Mayor John Fogg, Mayor Mike Wiggins, and Mayor Ashton Hayward III. Also, thanks to the four chairs who oversaw the Community Maritime Park Associates (CMPA), a subgroup who oversaw the construction of the park and the stadium: Judge Lacey Collier; Eddie Todd; James J. Reeves, Esq.;

and Collier Merrill, CMPA chairman. Finally, thanks goes to the various city council members and the members of the CMPA.

A special thanks goes to city council members John Fogg, P.C. Wu, J.D. Smith, Mike DeSorbo, John Jerralds, Jewel Cannada-Wynn, Ronald Townsend, Jack Nobles, and Mike Wiggins for voting yes on the project and hanging in there.

Thank you to the workgroup of the late Vice Admiral Jack Fetterman, Mayor Emeritus Vince J. Whibbs Sr., Dickie Appleyard, Raad Cawthon, Ellis Bullock, Miller Caldwell Jr., Bob Hart, and Mort O'Sullivan. Thanks also to Nancy Fetterman, who joined the group in Jack's place after he passed away.

As I think back over this workgroup, I am reminded of a story that showcases just how dedicated they were. Before the vote on the referendum, everyone was working hard to inform people on the Community Maritime Park. I had heard that a person was going to vote against the park. I was going on TV and couldn't get out to meet with this person. I called Mort to see if he could go see this person. Like he does, Mort said, "Of course." He called the person and made an appointment to see him. It was about 7:00 p.m. In a terrible rainstorm, Mort drove to his house. As he was pulling into the driveway, he noticed the garbage containers. The colors of the containers revealed whether the resident of the home was a city resident or lived outside the city limits. Like many old cities, the city limit lines wander. As Mort pulled up to the house, he saw that this person was just outside the city limits and therefore could not vote on the referendum. Still, Mort got out of his car, got drenched by rain, and spent time explaining the project and answering questions. He also shared with this person that he would not have a vote. That is Mort, a true trooper for the greater good.

Thank you to my daughters, Bekki Kennedy for her work on the Janesville business challenge, and Mallory Studer for her work with getting the Community Maritime Park referendum passed.

There are so many more to thank as well.

Thanks to the many businesses that hung in there before 2004 and after Hurricane Ivan.

To the many sponsors and donors to the Blue Wahoos and the Studer Community Institute.

To Bruce Baldwin, who pushed to see if we could get an affiliated team for Pensacola.

To the area media, specifically the *Pensacola News Journal*, *Independent News*, *Navarre Press*, and *Gulf Breeze News*, which, despite difficult financial times for the newspapers, continue to provide valuable local news. Thanks also to the radio stations in Pensacola: 1370 AM, especially the morning team of Jim Sanborn and Don Parker, 1620 AM, 790 AM, and 97.1 FM The Ticket. Also, thanks goes to 1330 AM in Milton, FL, and the television stations WEAR-TV 3, BlabTV, and WSRE public TV.

To Randy Hammer, from the early days at *PNJ* to his later connection with Gannett newspapers in Asheville, NC, to his service as the first CEO of Studer Community Institute until 2016. Randy has been on this journey since day one.

I would like to thank my home office team of Scott Remington, Randall Wells, and Mort O'Sullivan.

To Pensacola native Joe Scarborough of *Morning Joe*, for his kind words about Pensacola and his Blue Wahoos bobblehead.

Special thanks to Brian Spencer for his help with the chapter on government.

To the Downtown Improvement Board, who each day do their best to take positive actions to create a better community.

To the University of West Florida and Pensacola State College who have always been so helpful.

We are so grateful to Dr. John List and Dana Suskind, MD, and to the University of Chicago for the Thirty Million Words partnership. With this we can change the world.

To Impact100 for their support in implementing our early learning program.

Thanks also to Sandi Kemp from Navarre Press, Sherry Fundin, and Michael Ryan. They meticulously went through the advance reader's proof of this book and marked suggested changes. Their time and attention to detail are appreciated.

To Dr. Karl Lewis and Commissioner Lumon May for their role in founding "Living the Dream and a Tribute to Motown"—which celebrates Dr. Martin Luther King Jr.'s legacy—and the various Living the Dream Award recipients.

Thanks also to the CivicCon Steering Committee: D.C. Reeves, Travis Peterson, Dan Lindemann, Christian Wagley, Chris Aghayan, Will Dunaway, Jarah Jacquay, Lisa Nellessen-Savage, and Kevin Robinson.

To the fans of the Blue Wahoos and the customers of the Bodacious Family of Shops and Bubba's Sweet Spot. Tenants and residents with Studer Properties, your loyalty is appreciated.

To all the staff of the Studer Family of Companies whose engagement is so great. I would like to thank the Studer Community Institute staff and the volunteers who are so giving of their time and talent to the Early Brain Development Program, especially Madrina Ciano, Michelle Salzman, and Danny Zimmern. Thanks to all Studer Community Institute donors, sponsors, partners, and speakers for their support and investment in our community.

To the Studer Community Institute Board of Directors: Cindi Bear Bonner, Becca Boles, Patrick Elebash, Randy Hammer, Chad Henderson, Gail Husbands, Stacy Keller Williams, Jean Pierre N'Dione, Lisa Nellessen-Savage, Mort O'Sullivan, Janet Pilcher, Scott A. Remington, Martha Saunders, Julie Sheppard, Josh Sitton, and Bruce Watson, along with past Chairman Jerry Maygarden.

Also, thanks to the Pensacola Young Professionals for their support in getting the vote passed for the Community Maritime Park and overseeing the quality of life survey.

Robert Hill from WRNE was instrumental in getting the minority community fully engaged, and, for that, I'm grateful.

Special thanks to all the great service clubs in the Pensacola area. You do so much for our community.

To the many philanthropists who donate to a number of great causes. A special thanks goes to the Bear, Levin, Switzer, and McMillan families.

To Bubba and Angie Watson for their contributions to the community.

We appreciate all the people from the small business community who attend small business roundtables, monthly workshops, EntreCon, and CivicCon, as well as their speakers and presenters.

Thank you to the judges of the Pensacola Business Challenge: John Myslak, Rus Howard, Caron Sjoberg, John Peacock, Robert Hill, Richard Hawkins, PhD, and Andrew Rothfeder. Thanks also to those who judged the Janesville, WI,

Business Challenge: David Bagley, James Caldwell, Duffy Dillon, Deborah Adams, Brian Donnelly, Russ Kashian, Terri Miland, Alicia Reid, Joe Quaerna, Oakleigh Ryan, and Joe Scanlin.

Thanks also to Dan Shugart, sports director, and Steve Nissim, both with WEAR-TV; and Bill Vilona, columnist with *PNJ* Sports. They have been key contributors since 2002 with the Pensacola Pelicans and the Blue Wahoos.

To Bubba Watson, Charlie Ward, Justin Gatlin, Josh Sitton, Doug Baldwin, Reggie Evans, Michelle Snow, Derrick Brooks, Fred Robbins, Alfred Morris, Emmitt Smith, Lawrence Tynes, Derrick "Smoke" Gainer, Graham Gano, Joe Durant, Jerry Pate, Roy Jones Jr., the Armstrong brothers, Boo Weekley, Heath Slocum, Greg Litton, Damarious Randall, Addison Russell, and Ben Lively. They are great athletes and even better people in their dedication to making life better for others in Pensacola.

To Jerry Pate with Jerry Pate Turf & Irrigation Inc., a well-known professional golfer who runs a great business. While many teams have rainouts, the Wahoos rarely do thanks to the irrigation system that Jerry and his company installed.

To the 2015 Pensacola City Council and Escambia County Commissioners who helped to make Southtowne Apartments become a reality.

To all the healthcare organizations I've worked with over the past 30 years. They taught me it is possible to move a big needle!

To the friends of Bill W. Without you in this journey of recovery nothing would be possible. You are the greatest teachers in this classroom called life.

So many people have come together to make Pensacola a wonderful place to work, live, and play. It would be impossible to list them all. Please know that you are all appreciated and loved. Together, may we make our community better and better with each passing year.

Covenant for the Community

Workforce Diversification Plan for

_____

Office Project Located at_____,

Pensacola, FL

Memorandum of Understanding

This Workforce Diversification Plan describes the goals and processes for maximizing the utilization of Minority, Women, and Local Business Enterprises in, and the training and employment of local residents for the _____development in Pensacola, Florida. This Plan has been drafted and adopted by _____in cooperation with the undersigned partnering contractors. The Plan establishes goals and procedures for meaningful economic inclusion and the parties agree to review the Plan and assess the effectiveness of its implementation as the Project continues. Amendments may be made from time to time when the parties agree that enhancements would be beneficial.

On behalf of _____

_____ Date _____

By: _____

On behalf of _____

_____ Date _____

By: _____

PURPOSE

The parties to this Workforce Diversification Plan for _____ (the **"Plan"**) are united in their efforts to ensure, to the extent commercially reasonable, that ALL individuals, regardless of race, color, religion, age, gender, national origin, ancestry, creed, union membership, sexual orientation, or disability will have the maximum opportunity to be involved in significant ways in the construction of _____ (the **"Project"**). The parties are also united in realizing that the people who live in **Escambia and Santa Rosa Counties** and particularly within the **City of Pensacola**, where the Project is located, should share in the prosperity generated by the construction of the Project as an economic engine.

This plan establishes goals and methods for maximizing minority inclusion and local resident employment at the Project.

- This Plan shall be attached to all Project solicitations. All contracts and subcontracts entered into by _____ shall contain the Plan's inclusion goals and reporting responsibilities.

DISADVANTAGED BUSINESS Inclusion Goals

The following overall Project procurement goals have been established:

Construction	20% MBE	5% WBE

Minority and Woman Owned Business inclusion will be reported in two separate manners: as a fixed monetary value for M/WBE contracting based on the final project budget, and on a man-hours basis via the tracking of employees performing work on the project. The percentages listed above are presented for reference as ALL BIDDERS on the Project will be expected to contribute to _____ effort to comply with the Plan.

Methods FOR MEETING DISADVANTAGED BUSINESS Inclusion Goals

Prime Contractors, Subcontractors, and other business entities that are awarded Project contracts ("**Contractors**") shall use their best practical efforts to meet or exceed the established Disadvantaged Business Inclusion goals.

- Bidders that exceed the stated hiring goals may be given priority consideration.

- Contractors who submit proposals as joint ventures in a mentor-protégé relationship may be given priority consideration for contact awards.

Each Contractor shall prepare and submit to _____, a detailed inclusion plan that identifies its own ownership composition, its own scope of work, any part of that scope it intends to subcontract, and how it intends, through subcontracting, joint venturing, or using vendors and suppliers, to meet the established inclusion goals. A meeting is encouraged with the Diversity Administrator (as described in Article VIII of this Plan) during the course of preparation of the Contractor inclusion plan.

- The template for the Contractor's Workforce Diversification Plan is included as Exhibit A.

Each Contractor issuing solicitations for subcontracts or purchase orders shall take actions to ensure that Contracts will be awarded and administered in accordance with good faith and in the best interest of the overall goal of workforce diversification on this project.

Establishing Good Faith Best Practical Efforts

If any Contractor's Workforce Diversification Plan does not meet or exceed the established goals, the Contractor should prepare an analysis showing how it has made a good faith "best effort" to achieve the project goals. This analysis should include, but not be limited to, the following:

- Solicitation through newspapers, advertisements, job fairs, etc.;

- Correspondence between the Contractor firm and any MBE/WBE firms;

- Logs of phone calls to M/WBE firms listed in the City of Pensacola, Escambia County, or Santa Rosa County directories;

- Bid results and reasons why insufficient M/WBE awards were made.

_____ expects each Contractor to put forth good faith effort to meet or exceed the overall goals.

Non-Discrimination IN CONTRACTING AND HIRING Policy

Each Contractor performing work or providing goods or services shall ensure that it, along with its Subcontractors, shall not discriminate on the basis of race, color, religion, age, gender, national origin, ancestry, creed, union membership, sexual orientation, or disability in the award and performance of its contract and/or any sub-contracts that may be needed to perform the work or services for which they are contracted. Likewise, Contractor shall ensure that it, along with its Subcontractors, shall not discriminate on the basis of race, color, religion, age, gender, national origin, ancestry, creed, union membership, sexual orientation, or disability in the Project with respect to all employment practices. The Contractor shall comply with all applicable requirements of any federal, state or local law ordinance or regulation relating to affirmative action, equal opportunity and nondiscrimination in employment, and shall use its best practical efforts to meet all local goals relating thereto.

RESIDENT INCLUSION GOALS

In addition to the above-referenced overall contracting and non-discrimination goals established for the Project, the parties to this Plan voluntarily agree to work together so that, to the greatest extent within the limits of commercial reasonableness, individuals who reside in **Escambia and Santa Rosa County, Florida** (hereafter, "**Local Residents**") shall be preferred for hiring by the Contractors that work on the Project. Furthermore, the parties commit to collaborating on procedures to provide the necessary training for such work, as appropriate.

The overall employment goal established by this Plan shall apply to the total number of workers employed by a business winning a contract award for goods or services required for the design, construction, and management of the Project.

The minimum goal for employing Local Residents shall be 75% of all on-site employees.

In addition, this Plan establishes goals that apply to the number of new employees needed by a business winning a contract award for goods or services required for the design, construction, and management of the Project. Qualified Local Residents shall be given priority for employment under this agreement and will be considered before non- residents to be hired to fill new jobs created by this project.

The minimum goal for hiring Local Residents shall be 100% of all newly hired employees.

The objectives of this Plan are overall goals for the entire project and will not be evaluated on a contract by contract basis, although all Contractors and Subcontractors shall submit monthly manpower reports for the purpose of tracking Local Resident involvement in the Project.

Methods FOR MEETING LOCAL RESIDENT Economic Inclusion Goals

Persons or business entities that are awarded Project contracts ("**Contract Awardees**") shall use their best practical efforts to meet or exceed the established Local Resident Inclusion goals. Each Contract Awardee shall execute the Non-Discrimination in Hiring form attached hereto and made a part hereof as Exhibit B.

Each Contract Awardee shall schedule a meeting with _____ within two weeks of contract award. The meeting will provide the Awardee the opportunity to learn about the full range of workforce resources and employment related services available to them and to acquire assistance in developing its Manpower Projection Plan.

Each Contract Awardee shall submit a Manpower Projection Plan, using the form attached hereto and made a part hereof as <u>Exhibit C</u> no later than 30 days after contract award or 14 days prior to mobilization, whichever is earlier. The Manpower Projection Plan shall describe the general scope of the work under the Contract Awardee's contract, its total projected staffing, projected number of new hires, the type of skills and expertise needed for new hires that will be involved in fulfilling the contract and a timeline for commencing the work.

In the event that Contract Awardee's Manpower Projection Plan changes due to revisions in the scope of its contract or its approach to the work, the Contract Awardee should submit an update to its Plan to _____ as promptly as possible but in no event after commencement of the work.

Should the Contract Awardee's Manpower Projection Plan indicate a need to fill new jobs, the Contract Awardee should make notification through _____ for a period of fourteen (14) days prior to publicly advertising the openings. This will enable _____ to identify and refer qualified Local Residents to the Contract Awardee as candidates for these job opportunities. Public advertisements for job openings may appear in minority-owned media and non-minority-owned media.

No Contract Awardee will be required to hire personnel who are unqualified to fill job openings, however Contract Awardees are encouraged to consider opportunities for on-the-job training for qualified entry level workers.

Monitoring and Reporting

_____ shall monitor the Disadvantaged Business Inclusion and Local Resident hiring activity of the Contractors and submit monthly reports that document its progress to _____, **LLC.**

Disadvantaged Business Inclusion Reporting: Each Contractor with Subcontractors, suppliers, or vendors, shall provide the following information on a monthly basis with their Applications for Payment:

- A breakdown of all amounts billed for that month by Subcontractor and supplier indicating the M/WBE status of that Subcontractor or supplier;

- A contract-to-date summary of the total amount billed by each firm and presented showing the percentage of billings by M/WBE firms to the prime contract's value;

- Signed and notarized Affidavits of Total Payments to Date from each firm.

Any Contractor's failure to provide the monthly Subcontractor report could result in the delay of processing of the Contractor's Application for Payment.

Local Resident Inclusion Reporting: Manpower reports shall be submitted monthly by each Contractor, Subcontractor, and consultant with any workforce dedicated to the Project, along with request for payment.

Manpower reports shall include the name, address and zip code, and race of each employee dedicated to the Project, their job classification, and whether they are a new or existing employee.

All manpower reports will be compiled by _____ into an overall compliance statement, including copies of the individual manpower reports, and be forwarded to _____ monthly for review.

Any Contractor's failure to provide the monthly manpower report could result in the delay of processing of the Contractor's Application for Payment.

IMPLEMENTATION AND ADMINISTRATION

_____ has designated _____, during the construction of the Project as the Diversity Administrator, who shall be responsible for implementation of this Plan. The Diversity Administrator shall act as the primary coordinator of all aspects of this Plan and will be the primary point of contact for _____.

Coordinating with internal and external resources, the Diversity Administrator will be responsible for all implementation activities including the following:

- Disadvantaged Business Inclusion
  - Coordinate with Contractors on Project Scheduling and provide early notice of bidding schedules
  - Represent the Project at Contracting Expos and Pre-Bid Conferences
  - Monitor Contractor and Subcontractor bid advertising
  - Review and consolidate M/WBE Inclusion Plans from Contractors
  - Compose/submit required reports to _____

- Resident Inclusion
  - Coordinate with Contractors on Project Scheduling and provide advanced notice of Manpower Projections for planning of training and recruitment programs
  - Assist with identification of existing training programs that can be leveraged to help fill manpower needs, including sources of funding for worker training
  - Represent Project in interfacing with Contractors, Local Churches, Workforce Agencies, and Walk-Up Applicants
  - Review and consolidate Manpower Reports from Contractors
  - Compose/submit required reports to _____

More specific responsibilities may be developed as the project progresses to ensure the maximum effectiveness of the implementation of this Workforce Diversification Plan.

End of Document

Exhibits Follow

EXHIBIT A
CONTRACTOR'S WORKFORCE DIVERSIFICATION PLAN

The following shall constitute this Contractor's plan for satisfying the M/WBE contracting goals set forth in the Workforce Diversification Plan for _____. This information shall be provided for each trade or service that will be utilized for this project. Use additional sheets if necessary.

Name of Contractor: _____

Total Bid Amount: _____

Planned Overall M/WBE Participation (Goals) Include prime contractor's information, if applicable:				
Name of Contractor, Subcontractor, or Vendor	M/WBE Certification #	Trade, Service, Or Work to be Provided	Dollar Value	% Participation

The Subcontractors and vendors listed above ____ are or ____ are not (check one) currently under contract for the scope of work indicated. Actual M/WBE Inclusion will be monitored as part of the monthly Application for Payment so this Plan is submitted to indicate the means anticipated to achieve the inclusion goals.

Additional Comments:

_____

_____

_____

_____

_____

_____

_____

_____

_____

_____

By signing below, I attest that the above information is accurate to the best of my knowledge and that we will put forth our best practical efforts to achieve said participation goals.

_____   _____

Signature of Owner/Chief Executive Officer   Date

EXHIBIT B
CONTRACTOR AND SUBCONTRACTOR
ACKNOWLEDGEMENT FORM

Contractor is responsible for getting all Subcontractors to complete and sign this form. Please print out multiple forms as needed.

NON-DISCRIMINATION IN HIRING

NOTICE

The Contract Awardee and its Subcontractors shall not discriminate nor permit discrimination against any person because of race, color, religion, age, gender, national origin, ancestry, creed, handicap, sexual orientation, union membership, disabled or Vietnam era veteran status, or limited English proficiency in the performance of the contract, including, but not limited to, preparation, manufacture, fabrication, installation, erection and delivery of all supplies and equipment. In the event of receipt of such evidence of such discrimination by a Contract Awardee or its agents, employees or representatives, _____ shall have the right to terminate the Contract for cause. In the event of the continued refusal on the part of the Contract Awardee to comply with this anti-discrimination provision, the Contract Awardee may be removed from the list of approved bidders of _____.

The Contract Awardee agrees to include subparagraph (1) above with appropriate adjustments for the identity of the parties in all subcontracts, which are entered into for work to be performed pursuant to the Contract.

Trade Name of Prime Contractor: _____

_____ (Seal)

Signature of Prime Contractor Representative

or

Trade Name of Subcontractor: _____

_____ (Seal)

Signature of Subcontractor Representative

EXHIBIT C
MANPOWER PROJECTION PLAN

Contractor:		
Contract Scope:		
Total Bid Amount:	Start Date:	End Date:

Total # of Employees on Payroll:	Woman or Minority Owned Business:
☐ 0-50 ☐ 51-100 ☐ 101-150 ☐ 151-200+	☐ Yes ☐ No

Contractor Contact Information (person Responsible for working with
_____ **Company to achieve local hiring goals)**

Contact Name:		
Work Address:		
City:	State:	Zip:
Office Telephone:	Cell:	
Email Address:		

WORKFORCE PLAN

Projected Number of Required Workers for this entire project	Total Number of Current Employees on payroll	Projected Number of New Hires for this entire project

1. Is recruitment required for new hires by the Contractor?

    ☐ Yes   ☐ No   How soon? _____ days

2. If no, will former workers be brought back?

    ☐ Yes   ☐ No   How Many? _____

3. Is recruitment required for <u>any</u> of your Subcontractors?

    ☐ Yes   ☐ No

    If so, have them complete plan.

4. Does the Contractor have openings on other projects?

    ☐ Yes   ☐ No

5. If recruitment is required, complete chart below and attach job descriptions for each.

Position Title	# Jobs	Skills Required	Wage Rate	Experience Level (1=skilled, 2=entry, 3=no experience)

By signing below, I attest that the information above is accurate to the best of my knowledge and ensure that my company will put forth our best practical effort to hire local residents for all job openings available as a result of this project. This will assist to achieve the project hiring participation goals.

_____

Name of Authorized Contractor Representative

_____   _____

Signature of Authorized Contractor Representative   Date

Pensacola Metro Dashboard

The graphic below shows the 2017 Pensacola Metro Dashboard at a glance. We realize this has small type and is very hard to read! That's why, on the next several pages, you'll see much larger versions of each of the quality of life indicators.

The dashboard is posted on our website at www.studeri.org and updated as often as possible. See the chapter titled "Creating a Tailored Approach for Your City" to learn more.

Pensacola Metro
Dashboard

Objective benchmarks are vital to gauging progress
and identifying areas that need improvement

Preterm births

	Escambia County 2013-15	**12.8% of births** 1,478 babies	**Florida 10% of births** 65,744 babies
	Santa Rosa County 2013-15	**11.3% of births** 626 babies	

Escambia County ranks 62nd out of 67 counties in the preterm birth rate — and among 17 counties of similar population, Escambia ranked last. Santa Rosa County ranks 54th of 67 counties in terms of preterm births. Preterm birth rate tracks the percent of babies born before 37 weeks gestation. State health officials report the data as a three-year rolling rate.

VPK participation

	Escambia County 2015-16	**63.3%**	**Florida 78%**
	Santa Rosa County 2015-16	**67.3%**	

Since 2005, all Florida 4-year-olds have been eligible to attend voluntary prekindergarten for free. In Escambia County, during 2015-2016, 1,319 children who were eligible for the state program were not enrolled in it. In Escambia and Santa Rosa counties, participation rates lag behind the state rate.

Kindergarten readiness

	Escambia County 2013-14	**66.2%**	**Florida**
	Santa Rosa County 2013-14	**81.0%**	**71%**

This is the percentage of 5-year-olds found kindergarten-ready when evaluated in the first month of the school year. Children who are not ready for kindergarten may never catch up. This also puts extra stress on teachers and takes time away from other children. Problems with the state readiness screening process mean new rates haven't been issued for the last two years.

SOURCE: Florida Department of Education, Office of Early Learning
NOTE: Scoring reported differently beginning in 2010-2011.
Other states do not have comparable testing.

Free & reduced-price lunch

	Escambia County 2015-16 school year	**60.6%**	**Florida**
	Santa Rosa County 2015-16 school year	**45.3%**	**60.2%**

This helps measure poverty in a community. Children living in households at or below 185% of the poverty level are eligible to receive free or reduced-price meals at their schools.

SOURCE: Florida Department of Education

Cost of child care

	Escambia County	**49%** of a parent's monthly income	**Florida** **56%** of a parent's monthly income
	Santa Rosa County	**36%** of a parent's monthly income	

This tracks average child care costs (for infant and preschoolers) as a percentage of median income for single-parent families.

SOURCE: US Census Bureau / American Community Survey

Single-parent households

	Escambia County as of 2015	38% of families	Florida
	Santa Rosa County as of 2015	25.3% of families	36.7% of families

Children living in single-parent families often face more economic and social hurdles than their peers from two-parent families.

SOURCE: American Community Survey
NOTE: % is all households with single parents w/children divided by all households with children

High school graduation rate

	Escambia County 2015	76.1%	Florida
	Santa Rosa County 2015	85.7%	80.7%

This tracks the percentage of students who finished high school in four years.

SOURCE: Florida Department of Education

Crime rate

	Escambia County 2015	4,734.7 per 100,000 population	Florida
	Santa Rosa County 2015	1,292.6 per 100,000 population	3,300 per 100,000 population

This measures the number of crimes reported per 100,000 citizens, including both violent crimes and property crimes. One note: Among eight counties of roughly similar population, Escambia had the second highest violent crime rate per 100,000 — trailing only Leon County.

SOURCE: Florida Department of Law Enforcement

College graduates

	Escambia County 2015	24.5%	Florida 27.3%
	Santa Rosa County 2015	26.6%	

Research shows that communities with higher percentages of college-educated residents have higher wages overall. Pew Research Center study shows people with a college degree earned about $17,500 more a year than those with just a high school diploma.

SOURCE: Pew Research Center

Labor force participation

	Escambia County 2015	61.8%	Florida 59.2%
	Santa Rosa County 2015	59.8%	

The unemployment rate is often reported as a measure of joblessness, but it leaves out people who quit looking for work. Labor force participation shows how many people who are eligible to work are doing so.

SOURCE: US Census Bureau

Middle class households

	Escambia County as of 2015	64.5%	Florida 63.4%
	Santa Rosa County as of 2015	67.4%	

The percentage of households considered middle class in Escambia and Santa Rosa counties has remained relatively flat from 1990-2015, as has the state rate.

SOURCE: Woods and Poole Economics

Real per capita income

	Escambia County 2014	$36,632	Florida
	Santa Rosa County 2014	$37,610	$42,737

Real per capita income represents the total Gross Domestic Product (GDP) of our area, adjusted for inflation and divided by the population. It measures the average person's purchasing power and economic well-being.

SOURCE: US Bureau of Economic Analysis

Rent-burdened households

	Escambia County 2015	52.2%	Florida
	Santa Rosa County 2015	47.9%	58.3%

The rule of thumb for affordability is that housing should cost no more than 30% of your monthly income. This point tracks the percentage of people who spend more than that on rent.

SOURCE: American Community Survey

Population

	Escambia County from 2010 to 2015	+2.8%	Florida from 2010 to2015
	Santa Rosa County from 2010 to 2015	+6.0%	+4.2%

Data shows that after steeply increasing every decade between 1970 and 2000, the population stagnated. In 2015, Escambia County's population was 306,327; in Santa Rosa it was 161,021.

SOURCE: Woods and Poole Economics

Median workforce age

	Escambia County 2015	37.2	Florida 41.4
	Santa Rosa County 2015	39.5	

In 2015 in Escambia, the median workforce age was 37.2; in Santa Rosa it was 38. Florida was 41.4.

SOURCE: American Community Survey

Overweight and obesity rate

	Escambia County 2013	59.8%	Florida 62.8%
	Santa Rosa County 2013	60.9%	

Two out of three people in the Pensacola metro area are either overweight or obese, meaning they have a body mass index of 25 or higher. Obesity-related health problems diminish worker productivity and add cost to the health care system.

SOURCE: Florida Department of Health

Voter turnout

	Escambia County 2016	73.9% voters cast ballots	Florida 74.5% voters cast ballots
	Santa Rosa County 2016	68.1% voters cast ballots	

How healthy is democracy in your community? Voter turnout is one way to measure that.

SOURCE: Florida Department of State Division of Elections

Pensacola Metropolitan Statistical Area (MSA) includes all of Escambia and Santa Rosa counties in the state of Florida.

Notes

Chapter 3

1. Block, Peter. "Conversations for a Change." Designed Learning. http://www.designedlearning.com/about-designed-learning/articles-2/six-conversations-matter/conversations-for-a-change/.

Chapter 5

1. Clifton, Jim. *The Coming Jobs War*. Washington, DC: Gallup Press, 2011, 70.

Chapter 6

1. Seijts, Gerard, and Grace O. Farrell. "Engage the Heart: Appealing to the Emotions Facilitates Change." *Ivey Business Journal*, 2003. https://iveybusinessjournal.com/publication/engage-the-heart-appealing-to-the-emotions-facilitates-change/.

2. Ibid.

Chapter 7

1. Ruiz, don Miguel. *The Four Agreements: A Practical Guide to Personal Freedom*. San Rafael, CA: Amber-Allen Publishing, 1997.

Chapter 8

1. "The 20 Ingredients of an Outstanding Downtown." Destination Development Association. https://www.rogerbrooksinternational.com/20_Ingredients_Handout.pdf.

Chapter 9

1. "Neighborhoods First: A low risk, high return strategy for a better Brainerd." https://static.squarespace.com/static/53dd6676e4b0fedfbc26ea91/53ddcd89e4b003f5882015c4/53ddcd89e4b003f5882015c6/1383603482037/Neighborhoods%20First%20Report.pdf.

Chapter 10

1. Clifton, Jim. *The Coming Jobs War*. Washington, DC: Gallup Press, 2011, 67.

2. Benest, Frank. "Serving Customers or Engaging Citizens: What is the Future of Local Government?" *Public Management*, 1996.

Chapter 15

1. "Cities dream of wooing Amazon, but is it worth it?" *PBS NewsHour*. November 30, 2017. https://www.pbs.org/newshour/show/cities-dream-of-wooing-amazon-but-is-it-worth-it.

Chapter 17

1. Morioka, Erin. "Buy an existing business or start your own?" Yahoo Small Business. https://smallbusiness.yahoo.com/advisor/buying-existing-business-vs-starting-190019574.html.

2. Clifton, Jim. *The Coming Jobs War*. Washington, DC: Gallup Press, 2011, 74.

Chapter 18

1. Gates, Bill. "How Did Humans Get Smart?" *Gates Notes*, May 17, 2016. https://www.gatesnotes.com/Books/Sapiens-A-Brief-History-of-Human-kind.

About the Author

Quint Studer is founder of Pensacola's Studer Community Institute, a nonprofit organization focused on improving the community's quality of life and moving Escambia and Santa Rosa counties forward. He is a businessman, a visionary, an entrepreneur, and a mentor to many. He currently serves as the Entrepreneur-in-Residence at the University of West Florida.

Quint has given his life to designing the building blocks for people and organizations that guide them to achieving and sustaining high performance. In 2000 he founded a consulting firm designed to help organizations improve results. Over the years it won multiple awards, including the 2010 Malcolm Baldrige National Quality Award. By the time the firm was sold in 2015, it had 250 employees.

In addition to *Building a Vibrant Community: How Citizen-Powered Change Is Reshaping America*, Quint has authored seven books, including *Results That Last*, which reached number seven on the *Wall Street Journal* bestseller list. He writes a weekly employee development column that runs every Sunday in the *Pensacola News Journal*. All proceeds from *Building a Vibrant Community* will go toward Studer Community Institute's work in early brain development.

About the Studer Community Institute

The Studer Community Institute is focused on improving our community's quality of life by building a vibrant community.

The cornerstone of the institute's work is the community dashboard. These metrics provide a snapshot of the educational, economic, and social well-being of the community. The dashboard allows people to compare our community's performance to other similarly sized communities in measures ranging from high school graduation rates to household incomes.

Research indicates two areas that are key to an area's quality of life are jobs and education. The institute's research shows improving these two areas is crucial to improving the quality of life for all the citizens of the Pensacola metro area.

In education, the institute is focused on efforts to create America's first "Early Learning City" and boost kindergarten readiness. An Early Learning City is a place that enlists the whole community in building a culture of lifelong learning, including in its public spaces. It is a community that supports early brain development, parent engagement, and school readiness for all of our children, especially those ages birth to five.

In job creation and development, the institute provides leadership development training and sponsors workshops geared to help businesses and not-for-profits strengthen their organizations. Outreach programs include a lecture series, symposiums, and town hall meetings.

Our trainings offer important skill-building opportunities for small and medium-sized businesses, nonprofits, and entrepreneurs. With more skills, business owners and employees in turn create better-run organizations that are better positioned to thrive, create more jobs, and support a stronger community.

Our mission is to improve the quality of life by building vibrant communities.

The Studer Community Institute is a 501(c)(3) public charity (EIN 47-5657008) and is registered with the Florida Department of Agriculture and Consumer Services to solicit contributions (Registration #CH48388). Donors can deduct contributions under Internal Revenue Code Section 170.

A copy of the official registration and financial information may be obtained from the Division of Consumer Services by calling toll-free 800-435-7352 within the state. Registration does not imply endorsement, approval, or recommendation by the state.

Studer Community Institute

220 West Garden St., Suite 100

Pensacola, FL 32502

www.studeri.org

info@studeri.org

Notes

Notes

Notes

Notes

Notes

Notes